"

Using nature as our inspiration, we can look at our dog and understand their priorities, needs and desires. The goal of this book is to build your relationship with your dog by respecting their natural character, rather than fighting it.

"

$(Dog)^{10}$

An Intuitive 10-Step Training Program To Raise The Perfect Dog.

Designed By Dogs, For Dogs.

Written And Illustrated By:
Michele Caricato
Laura Di Marco
Stevo Dirnberger
Chanel Cartell

Written by: Michele Caricato, Laura Di Marco
Edited by: Stevo Dirnberger, Chanel Cartell, Dasia Lutova
Illustrations: Stevo Dirnberger
Cover and Interior Design: Chanel Cartell

ISBN 978-0-620-86168-7

Print on Demand & eBook Editions crafted with love by the team at www.myebook.online.

MYEBOOK
WE EMPOWER AUTHORS

CONTENTS

INTRODUCTION

It's like a bum sniff – but for humans

What is Dog to the Power of 10?

The (Dog)^{10} approach is based on the balance of various aspects that make up our dog's life (and ours).

Nature is a great teacher. It balances entire ecosystems, making sure each individual in a system has the right predispositions, abilities, and attitudes to contribute perfectly to the cohesive whole. Using nature as our inspiration, we can look at our dog and understand their priorities, needs and desires. The goal of this book is to build your relationship with your dog by respecting their natural character, rather than fighting it.

Don't worry, it's easier than you think!

To illustrate the point of every chapter, we'll follow the life of a wolf, from his very first steps outside the den to a rich life of hunting, socializing, and solving problems. We'll look at the world through his eyes and see what he can teach us about our dog's canine nature.

Once we start to understand our dog's motivations through their wolfish ancestry, we can start applying those lessons to teach them new behaviors, and improve their relationship to us and the world around them. You'll learn how to build your relationship with training exercises and activities you'll both enjoy.

The (Dog)^{10} approach is about more than just teaching commands and having a well-behaved dog. It's about ensuring your dog is emotionally and physically healthy, as their quality of life impacts your entire family. As you begin to meet their emotional, mental and physical needs, they will rise up to impress you in ways you'd never expect.

This book will take you on a journey of discovery. You'll find out more about your dog's inner world, and you'll probably find out something new about yourself as well.

To shake us out of our comfort zone and set us out on a journey, however, we need a catalyst.

In chemistry, a catalyst is a substance that increases the speed of a reaction. In a figurative sense, a catalyst is an individual, idea, or event which sparks your motivation and drives you to make a change in your life.

So, will this book be your catalyst?

Honestly? No. Your catalyst is probably right next to you, or by your feet, or chasing their tail in the garden right now.

Your dog is the reason you're reading this book. Your dog is a wonderful creature and, though they test your patience and upset your plans sometimes, they'll be the one to guide and inspire you on this journey.

What are you waiting for? Let's go!

STEP 1:

SOCIALIZATION

Being around fellow four-legged friends

The Origins of 'Socialization'

Stevo's life as a wolf cub begins with warmth and safety. Until now, Stevo's world has been contained in this warm and comfortable den, which he shares with his siblings and loving Mother Wolf. The Mother Wolf has spent most of her time looking after the cubs — feeding, cleaning and protecting them in the safety and darkness of their underground chamber.

But today, she is late to lunch. Stevo's patience is tested for the very first time. He is hungry, restless and confused. He plays with his sister, but it doesn't last long. There's only one thing on his mind — milk!

The moments of hunger stretch into minutes, and Stevo feels an over-whelming urge to go outside, beyond the safety of the den.

He scampers along the tunnel. The light gets brighter, and he squints his big eyes closed.

Suddenly, Stevo has reached the exit, and in an instant he's hit by a thousand different smells, sounds, and colors. He scoots back into the den to catch his breath, overwhelmed by the assault of new sensations.

Looking back over his shoulder, he can barely make out the outlines of his brothers and sisters cuddling together at the heart of the den.

"Hey guys!" Stevo yells, "Come look! There's something incredible out there!"

The other cubs stir and begin to move towards him, hesitating at the bright light. Stevo's curiosity surges through him, so he steps outside alone.

The first few moments outside are a rush. Stevo is suddenly petrified – he doesn't know where to look or how to feel. But one by one, his siblings cautiously join him, and he starts to relax.

He takes a few more steps forward, and there is something new beneath his paws: soft and fragrant grass, a world of difference from the dry earth he's spent his first few weeks of life on. He tries to look up, but the huge expanse of the sky leaves him feeling dizzy. In the distance, he sees a dark shape. A shape that's familiar, and coming closer and closer towards them.

It's Mother Wolf!

The cubs courageously head towards Mother Wolf, with Stevo leading the charge across the springy grass. Mother Wolf sniffs each of the cubs quickly to check they're alright, then lies down. The feeding frenzy begins.

Soon after lunch, the questions start:

"Mom! What's this?"

"And this?"

"Look at that!"

"Listen to this!"

The cubs' curiosity has no limits, and Mother Wolf gently guides them to explore this new world. Some cubs are overwhelmed, and run to hide between her feet, but she acts as if nothing has happened. She is calm and supportive, never reacting to their fear.

"If Mom's not scared, there's definitely no danger." Stevo thinks to himself before chasing a butterfly.

Suddenly, new creatures approach the playing cubs. They're like Mother Wolf, but each has a new and unfamiliar scent. These strangers are the Elders, and Stevo panics as one hovers over him. Luckily, Stevo remembers that Mother Wolf taught him to go belly-up in these sorts of situations. After a quick sniff, the stranger goes away.

"Guys, don't be afraid!" Stevo tells the other cubs, "Look, it's easy — you just need to do this, and no one will hurt you." he plops onto his back and shows his soft belly to them.

"Wow!" The other cubs start to practice the posture, turning it into a game and nipping each other in the belly when they get a chance.

Over the next few days, the cubs' explorations become longer. Though intimidating at first, the Elders are all very friendly and affectionate – though in Stevo's mind they're a little selfish, not sharing any milk with the cubs.

Mother Wolf is very methodical with her approach, allowing the cubs to walk further and further each day. She offers them help and security in difficult situations, but intervenes less and less over time. She's always attentive, but wants them to learn to fend for themselves. It's important they make mistakes and learn quickly from them.

With all the excitement of the outside world, as well as the exercise they get while exploring, the cubs get hungrier every day. Their diet begins to change from Mother Wolf's milk to small chunks of meat that Mother Wolf regurgitates for them.

"It's so tasty, but do you know how to drink it?" Stevo asks one of his sisters, poking the chunk with his nose, "I'm trying to suck, but it's not working."

"Don't suck, stupid!" His sister barks at him, "Open your mouth, then close your mouth. Like this," she shows him how to chew, stealing his portion in the process.

"Mom! Mom, she's eaten all my food!" moans Stevo.

But Mother Wolf calmly ignores his whines. She knows that she won't always be around to feed the cubs, so Stevo needs to wake up a little if he wants to survive.

Stevo's life is filled with exciting new experiences now, so he's focusing on more than just food. He's filled with constant urges to run and explore, try new tactics to knock his siblings down, and to socialize with the Elders.

"Sometimes, when the sky goes grey, I hear loud crashing noises," Stevo tells Aunt Wolf, "The first time I heard it I was terrified! I couldn't help but run into the den to hide. But now, I don't care about the noise. I just continue to play as if nothing ever happened." He says proudly.

"That's nice, dear." Aunt Wolf yawns.

Thanks to Mother Wolf's way of observing them closely, but without intervening or coddling, in a few short weeks the little cubs have become masters of many difficult situations. They've explored so far beyond the den that they're familiar with every rock and blade of grass in the area. They've learned to recognize real danger and know the difference between risk and simple fear. Most of all, they've learned to trust all the members of their pack.

What is 'Socialization' and how do you apply it as a dog owner?

Dogs are social animals, and much like human teenagers, they need certain experiences to understand where they fit into society. Every dog needs to interact with other dogs so that they can learn the rules of engagement, and understand how to relate to others using posture, attitude, and vocalization. They need to become familiar with the outside world and everything in it, including noises, objects, other animals and all sorts of situations. Your dog needs to discover the world piece by piece, and make positive associations along the way.

This process is called socialization. It's critical in the first few months of your puppy's life, as each day they add more experiences to their sense of how the world works, and how they should behave in it.

But socialization isn't just for puppies. In fact, it's equally important for adult dogs, so they can keep feeling balanced and connected to the world. Lack of socialization and stimulation early on in a dog's life will often lead to behavioral and social problems. This shows up as fear and distrust in puppies, and later becomes apathy, stress and aggression in adult dogs.

As a human, you have the tools to "socialize" and connect with the world at your fingertips. You can watch hundreds of TV channels, explore endless content on the internet, hop between dozens of apps, and chat to your friends through social media – all without leaving the couch.

Your dog, on the other hand, can't entertain themselves so easily. To feel connected and social, they need to get out, explore, and see what's going on in the world.
Your dog does in fact have plenty of 'channels' or 'apps' to choose from, but these are a little different to the ones we browse through…

- Other dogs: big, small, male, female, hairy, not-so-hairy.
- Humans: men, women, children (with two and four legs), and of course that odd sub-species – the mailman!
- Noises: classical music, modern hip-hop, thunder, fireworks.
- Various places and objects: the lawn, the lawn after a dog has been on it, garbage cans, stairs, the city center, the park around the corner, the ocean, bars, restaurants… The list is endless.

So, your dog needs to socialize and explore, but where do you fit in? What role should you play in the great discovery (and re-discovery) of their world? Ideally... none!

You are the Mother Wolf in your dog's world. As a good Mother Wolf, your role should be as neutral as possible, and your attitude always calm, collected, and detached.

Your dog instinctively feels that if you intervene in a situation, that situation must be incredibly dangerous – much like a Mother Wolf stepping in to rescue her cub from a bear. In fact, most dogs develop fears early in life, not from what we'd see as "traumatic experiences", but simply due to their owners intervening too much, and accidentally taking away their dog's self-confidence.

TIPS FOR 'SOCIALIZATION'

Scenario: During your walk, you spot a dog that looks unfriendly and you want to avoid a confrontation.

- **DON'T:** Pick up your dog out of fear.
- **DO:** Walk away quietly, allowing your dog to follow you on the leash.

Scenario: Your dog is barking furiously at a stranger.

- **DON'T:** Pet your dog or try to calm them down, because next time they will only bark louder.
- **DO:** Move in front of your dog confidently, making them understand that you have the situation under control.

Scenario: Thunder, or any other sudden loud noises.

- **DON'T:** Reassure your dog saying, "it's just a storm, it will be ok."
- **DO:** Have no reaction at all, pretending they were the only one who heard the noises.

Scenario: Your dog is afraid of a gutter, or some other objects on your walk.

- **DON'T:** Avoid it, or try to coddle or soothe your dog once you get near it.
- **DO:** Come prepared with a ball or toy. When you get to the offending area, distract your pooch with a game, staying calm and lighthearted the entire time.

'SOCIALIZATION' PUT INTO PRACTICE

The perfect socialization program lets your dog have varying experiences, alternating between stressful and calm sessions. For puppies, it's important to alternate the challenging sessions with relaxing, predictable experiences.

Here's a sample week of socialization sessions:

- **Monday:** A day at the park to play with friends.
- **Tuesday:** A walk in the city center.
- **Wednesday:** A day at the park to play with friends.
- **Thursday:** A day at the mall.
- **Friday:** A day at the park to play with friends.
- **Weekend:** Somewhere completely new, like a forest or a lake.

At this point, it's best to draw up a short list of potential difficulties for your dog, that you can work on during and between sessions.

Some of these socialization obstacles might be:

Busy places like markets, main roads, or shopping centers

Before you arrive at a new or potentially scary place, try to take a twenty-minute walk beforehand, then stroll through the busy place imagining that you were in the countryside. Act as if nothing is happening, and pretend not to see the chaos around you, especially ignoring anything that bothers your furry friend. Don't look at your dog, and resist speaking to them. To make it easier, try picking a landmark in front of you (for example the entrance of a store) and focusing on that point. Simply stroll and stay calm. The first session shouldn't last more than five minutes, and it would be best not to exceed two or three sessions per week. Increase these 'stressful' sessions by five minutes as you make progress.

Scary noises

If your dog is easily spooked by noise, technology will be your best friend. Get recordings of disturbing noises (such as sirens, loud bangs or thunder), and play them during normally pleasant times for your dog, for example, when you are preparing their food. Begin with the volume quite low during the first few sessions. The secret is to always ignore the noise yourself, and let the dog believe that they're the only one who can hear it! As you remain indifferent, your dog learns to stay calm.

11

People

This is slightly more difficult to organize, as you'll need to find willing volunteers with the right attitude – that attitude of cool indifference towards your dog. If done correctly, these exercises can prove to be highly beneficial. The best exercise is to walk casually up to someone whose back is turned towards you, making sure your dog touches him or her as you pass by. Another exercise (if you have a group of patient friends) would be to create the 'circle of friendship' - you have your helpers (four or more) three meters away from you, standing in a circle around you and your dog. In turn, each of your friends calls the dog, gives them a treat, and then turns away immediately (it's important that your friends don't interact with your dog, and look at them as little as possible — they're simply food dispensers).

Each of these situations mentioned above are great practical exercises that help socialize your dog.

'Socialization' Case Study: Bella Learns Bravery

MEET BELLA

Bella is the sweetest and most affectionate dog you'll ever meet. She's a French Bulldog who lives with her owner, Emily. Bella comes from a shelter, because her previous owners grew tired of her after only a few weeks.

When Emily spotted her on an adoption site, she immediately needed to meet Bella! When they met, it was love at first sight for them both. Bella, who was six months old at the time, was completely smitten. Within minutes, she switched from being a quiet introvert sitting in a corner of the shelter, to a happy and excited puppy who was ready for life with her new family.

The first few days at Bella's new home, however, were not easy. Bella was afraid of every noise she heard. Every time Emily made a sudden movement, Bella would dash into her bed to hide. Going out for a walk was worse — Bella would tremble with every step, and would go belly-up every time she met a new person or, heaven forbid, a new dog. Emily started feeling desperate. She wondered if she'd made the right decision by adopting Bella.

Luckily, due to her patience, things at home began to improve. Bella became calmer when it was just the two of them at home. Then, as new guests started to visit, they would befriend the shy dog by offering her scraps of food from the table. Bella began to happily welcome guests, although still with some hesitation, and often leaving a few drops of urine on the carpet.

Outside of home, however, Bella's skittish behavior went from bad to worse. Emily began having issues with Bella before they were even out the door. Bella would stop at the door and refuse to go out. Once outside, Bella would shake and stop repeatedly in the middle of the street, pulling Emily back towards home.

Emily was doing her best, but ironically, all the protective attention she gave Bella made the entire situation worse. Emily even let Bella sleep with her to comfort the anxious dog. And while the treats from Emily's friends had a positive effect on Bella at home, they also taught the dog that acting shy and fearful would be rewarded with food.

Though all the humans in Bella's life had the best intentions, they were sending the wrong message altogether.

BELLA'S RECOVERY PROGRAM

Bella's recovery program relied on one huge change: Emily's attitude. Her maternal and instinctual behavior to 'protect the sweet puppy' actually made Emily seem fragile in Bella's eyes. Emily's love had turned to pity, and Bella's growing helplessness left Emily feeling guilty and inadequate.

- Firstly, Emily needed to regain her self-esteem, believing in her capacity to be a good dog owner, and remembering how lucky Bella was to be rescued from the shelter.

- She then needed to detach her actions from her emotions. That meant stopping all pitiful looks, and drastically reducing the amount of attention Bella received at home (both from Emily, and from her friends). Everyone needed to act indifferently when Bella appeared agitated or troubled, and to completely ignore her when they came into the house. Bella's nervous peeing disappeared after day one, and she only received small treats when she was calm and lay beside the table.

- For the walks outside, Emily needed to create a new ritual. She would begin by taking Bella outside on the leash, and meeting a friend at the gate. The friend would then take the leash, and Emily would walk ahead. The first time, Bella hesitated, torn between the desire to go back home to hide, versus following her owner, who was headed in the opposite direction. Luckily, after a little while Bella chose to follow Emily.

Below you can see the diary of Bella's five-day recovery plan:

- **Day 1:** Bella and Emily meet a friend at the gate, and the friend takes the leash. Emily walks 30 meters ahead and waits for Bella and her friend to catch up. Then they all walk together for another five minutes, with the friend holding the leash the entire time.

- **Day 2:** Same as Day 1.

- **Day 3:** Bella, Emily and her friend go for a five-minute walk, all walking altogether. Emily's friend is still the person holding the leash.

- **Day 4:** Same as Day 1.

- **Day 5:** Bella and Emily's friend follow a bit behind Emily as she walks, then once they reach her, Emily would take the leash and they would all walk together for five minutes.

The best part about the new ritual was that Bella was more concerned with getting to Emily that she forgot to be afraid. Emily, in turn, was too busy with the ritual to think about Bella's reactions.

In the following weeks, they tweaked the walking ritual as follows:

- After the usual walking routine from their first week, Emily would take the leash and continue walking (without looking at Bella) for ten minutes – just enough time to get to the park. Then they would turn around and go back home

- Soon, Emily's friend was phased out of the ritual altogether.

- The walks were extended to include some time hanging around the park entrance, and in the area where dogs can roam free, although Bella remained on the leash.

- To complete the recovery, Emily had to prove her love for Bella by giving her some independence. They entered the free-roam section of the dog park, and Bella would be let off her leash. When other dogs would approach Bella, Emily would have to take a newspaper, open it, and read it! This was tough at first, and Emily even resorted to crying out of fear that something awful might happen. But she persevered, and even ended up enjoying her newspaper a little.

BELLA'S HAPPY ENDING

After three days at the dog park, Bella made friends with a Golden Retriever and a Dachshund, and a week later she was pulling on the leash to go play with her friends! Within a month, she had no fear of new people in the park either.

Soon after, Emily began to follow the socialization plan for herself! She realized that she wasn't too comfortable with public places, and that fear must have rubbed off on Bella. Emily got out of the house more, opting to go out to dinner instead of only inviting friends over to her home. She also got a promotion at work because she gained confidence, stopped living in the shadows, and began to take credit when it was due.

So, did Emily rescue Bella, or vice versa? We'll never know.

STEP 2:

LIVING IN A PACK

Understanding who is the leader, and who is not

The Origins of 'Living in a Pack'

A few days have passed since Stevo first left the den, and while he's getting to grips with the world at large, some of the other Elders in the pack are still a mystery to him. Even though they all look the same, Stevo starts to notice their different scents and how they act – strangely, but consistently. His biggest challenge now is to understand how these beings work.

With Mother Wolf it's easy — she's always clear with what she wants, and she always takes the time to explain things to her cubs. But with the others, it's a little difficult for Stevo to judge.

He thinks to himself:

"There's this sweet and helpful female Elder who often stays close to us and watches us when Mother Wolf is away... she's nice!"

"Then there's another Elder, who seems nice from far, but he's always digging holes, and he growls at me when I approach him."

"Oh, and then there's this majestic Elder — the one that sits on the hill. He's definitely the most striking, and the most fascinating. He's the guardian, always watching over the whole pack and everything around us. When he walks among the other Elders, they all show him affection. It's like they all love him! Sometimes I'm afraid of him, but I don't actually know why...."

Stevo's curiosity is endless, so today he decides to take advantage of a rare moment when Mother Wolf isn't watching. He sneaks off with his sister to go up the hill where that mighty, intimidating Elder sits.

"Are you sure it's safe?" whines his little sister, anxiously looking back, "Mom said we mustn't stray too far away from the den!"

But Stevo is very determined.

"It's only a little way away — what could go wrong? He's a member of our pack, and if he can go up there, it means we all can!"

"I don't think it works like that," his sister replies warily, "Who taught you that rule?"

"Oh, come on!" Stevo nudges her forward, "Don't worry so much! Can't you see how epic he looks up there? When I grow up, I want to be just like him!"

As they edge up the hill behind him, Alpha Wolf stands up, stretching a little whilst looking at the two small fugitives. Then he turns away and walks off quietly.

In a flash, Mother Wolf gathers the two naughty cubs, and herds them back into the safety zone of the den.

"Mom! Mom! Who is that guy? And why does he never come to cuddle us?" little Stevo asks excitedly.

"He will cuddle you when you become a little more disciplined, obeying your mother and the rules," she responds. "Alpha Wolf is the wisest and strongest wolf in our pack," she continues, "he's the one we turn to for guidance. He helps us all survive, always knows where to find good food, and how to defend us from danger."

"Yeah but... he's pretty selfish," Stevo's sister mumbles, "He always eats first, and he always wants to be in front of everyone else."

"Of course he eats first," Stevo snaps at her. "Can't you see he's the boss of all the wolves?!"

"No," Mother Wolf corrects him, "he eats first because he's our leader, our pack's guiding light, and the one we turn to when we're unsure. By having him eat first, we show him respect and gratitude for everything he does for us."

Mother Wolf gives each of her cubs an affectionate rub, and leaves them to play by themselves.

That night, as his brothers and sisters are snoozing around Mother Wolf, Stevo can't stop thinking about the majestic figure on the hill. Alpha Wolf is so heroic, he's like the heart of the pack. Stevo sees now why all the wolves gravitate towards him, and why they have so much respect for him.

"Starting tomorrow," Stevo whispers to himself, "I'm going to do everything I can to be just like him."

What is 'Living in a Pack' and how do you apply it as a dog owner?

Dogs are hyper-social animals. One of the biggest desires for any dog is feeling like they are a part of a group. That group could be all-canine, such as our wolf pack, or in the case of domestic dogs, a mix of human and canine.

Clarity is critical. This group needs to have all the relationships, tasks and responsibilities well defined. Each group member's limits and privileges are clear and unambiguous. Having a guiding light that defines group dynamics is actually a basic need for every dog.

Your dog will instinctively study the group they're in and choose the figure that appears to be the pack leader – the Alpha. The one that will ensure the survival and well-being of the entire group.

So, who will be the Alpha? Your dog will naturally gravitate towards an authoritative person. One who is always calm, determined, self-confident, and is able to manage their life without being overwhelmed by negative emotions. A good leader also clearly communicates their expectations of others, knows who to trust, and delegates tasks instead of doing everything themselves.

Physical strength and aggressiveness won't guarantee a good leader, nor will the qualities of irritability, laziness and impatience. While there may be some violent bouts in nature, (less than you think, but it happens) those fights are nothing compared to the moments of collaboration. An Alpha Wolf doesn't attack a pack member because they failed to take down the prey, or didn't chase it correctly, or lost the track. He works with them, and guides them to do better next time.

How can we, as pack leaders, work on improving our dog's sense of belonging?

TIPS FOR 'LIVING IN A PACK'

Attitude

The way you behave with a dog that is anxious, insecure and apprehensive is hugely important. If you want to help them, then you need to ignore the dog when they're in this negative state. Giving attention will be perceived as approval of their behavior.

If you're calm and patient, you can teach them the right way to react in times of stress and anxiety. When the dog calms down, you can show them all the enthusiasm and affection you want. This way, your pooch will fall in love with you, viewing you as their leader.

Places

Define from the beginning where your dog is allowed and where they're forbidden. This will easily reduce their rank in the pack, and let them see you as the leader making territorial decisions.

There are no standard rules for this, it will depend on the type of dog you have, their nature and temperament. If your dog is quite dominant, it'll be more necessary to restrict them, but if you have a docile little angel, it won't be a problem to let them sleep with you.

It's important to understand that every place has a certain amount of value in your dog's mind, so act accordingly. "Territories" from most to least important:

- » The bed, the bedroom, the sofa
- » Next to the dining room table, the kitchen, the living room
- » Inside the house
- » The garden
- » A certain part of the garden

Food

Food is probably the most important factor affecting your dog's behavior. Their instinctual need to hunt for food includes a series of activities, namely: searching, chasing, capturing, killing and eating. All of this requires a lot of time and energy, and that is why food is the most important part of an animal's life.

The modern dog is lucky – they don't need to wake up early to go hunting! But much like our human reliance on fast food, this convenience can cause unpleasant side effects later.

Firstly, we must understand that your dog's natural cycle is to hunt before eating. Simply serving food disturbs this cycle, confusing your dog. If you panic and worry about them eating, it makes matters worse. Of course, the pack leader ensures everyone has enough food - but the angst and stress you exude if your dog doesn't eat is counterproductive. You weaken your leaderships position by allowing your dog to dictate your mood and behavior through food.

If your dog doesn't eat, you might panic and begin looking for a solution – adding something to the food, changing it, even begging them to eat! But catering to your dog's whims isn't the right approach.

Setting up rules around food is imperative to your dog's sense of a balanced pack life. That's why you should always apply this age-old rule: leave the bowl of food in front of your dog for no more than twenty minutes*, and then take it away, whether it's full or empty. It's crucial not to try make the food more appealing for them if they don't want to eat.

*Some breeders will leave food out for puppies all the time as a form of training, teaching them to eat slowly and not be greedy — this is a different matter and does not apply to the above twenty-minute rule.

Physical Contact

Many dogs interpret our physical contact with them (cuddles and petting) as a weakness, but that doesn't mean you should never show your dog affection! In fact, to help your dog understand right and wrong, you must use enthusiasm and positive actions, such as cuddles, to reward their correct behavior.

However, if you give cuddles or show affection at the wrong times, you might accidentally weaken your leadership position, and cause some behavioral disorders.

Guiding Movements

The pack leader decides how the pack needs to move: where, when, and in which direction. However, if your dog is always in front of you during a walk, this does not automatically make them the leader. In fact, your dog is just the "chief of walks" and we, as pack leaders, assign this task to our dog - we are still very much in control.

The fundamental difference is the decision-making element. Are you picking the path, or are you at the mercy of your furry friend? As usual, it's your attitude and sense of control that decides the outcome.

'LIVING IN A PACK' PUT INTO PRACTICE

Here's a quick exercise to evaluate your dog's behavior.
On a scale of 1 to 5, rate your dog's behavior:

1. **Impossible to handle** – they're in charge, and if you don't obey, they become an absolute menace.
2. **Disobedient and independent** – they do whatever they want.
3. **Balanced** – in some situations they're an angel, but sometimes they're a little hard to handle.
4. **Lovely and obedient** – in most situations, inside and outside, they're a well-behaved dog.
5. **Calm, flexible and always friendly** – they love to work with you, can follow you anywhere, and are always perfectly behaved.

On a scale of 1 to 5, rate your relationship with your dog:

1. **Emotionally oversensitive** – the thought of something hurting your dog, or your dog not having everything, makes you go crazy. If they don't eat or act normally, you instantly panic.
2. **Desperate** – you try to educate your dog, but it's exhausting. You often have meltdowns and scold them. You're frustrated, and can't understand why they doesn't obey, even though you keep correcting them and giving commands.
3. **At a stalemate** – you've found a way to live with your dog, accepting their character flaws without trying to change their behavior.
4. **Patient, but firm** – your dog gladly follows you around, and you're interested in improving your relationship. You respect their natural instincts.
5. **Blissful and rewarding** – you interact with your dog in a calm and productive way. You're not overly sensitive and the two of you enjoy many activities together.

On a scale of 1 to 5, rate yourself in a work environment:

1. **A push over** – you often hide and prefer to suffer in silence.
2. **Tend to avoid confrontation** – you never complain, but at home you're anxious and angry, because the injustices at work are still brewing inside you.
3. **Undervalued** – you are calm and passive, but don't often get what you deserve.

4. **Successful** – you are well respected and feel like your life is heading in the right direction.
5. **A great leader** – you are admired and appreciated. People describe you as kind, attentive, and as someone who naturally commands respect.

You can reach your own conclusion after this exercise. What you may notice is your scores on all three questions are either the same, or very similar.

If you scored your dog's behavior and your relationship low on the scale, you might notice your own score at work is nowhere near a five. It's a tough question, but it might be time to ask yourself: "If I were a dog (or a wolf), would I blindly trust and follow a person like me?"

'Living in a Pack' Case Study: Max Learns His Place

MEET MAX

After years spent studying and doing internships, Noah had finally started working at a prestigious law firm, and had settled in a small house just outside of town. He finally had the opportunity to fulfill his life-long dream: owning a Rottweiler.

When Noah was a child, he'd spent many summers at the lake with his family, staying with his uncle and bonding with his uncle's Rottweiler. Noah spent most of his time playing with this gentle giant. Since then, he had always kept those wonderful feelings of warmth, joy and affection in his mind. So as soon as he had the opportunity, he would be getting himself this beautiful breed too.

Enter Max!

The first two months with Max were a bit challenging, because the puppy needed more time than Noah could dedicate to him. But Noah was determined to make it work, and hired a dog sitter to look after Max when he wasn't there. Problem solved.

After their daily walk, Noah and Max spent the evenings relaxing, often falling asleep on the couch watching TV. Sometime in the night, Noah found strength to get up and go to the bedroom, followed by his faithful friend, who had his bed right next to his owner's.

Their life was fairly predictable and fun, and it became even more exciting when they spent their holidays in the house on the lake. Noah was very proud to present the puppy to his family, who all grew up with the Rottweiler Noah played with as a little boy.

Max and Noah had a great summer. They enjoyed three weeks together at the lake house, living and playing side by side, 24 hours a day.

In September, when they returned to their home and to their routine, Noah got a nasty surprise. At work, he got a call from the dog sitter saying that Max had growled at him during feeding, and that he couldn't get close to Max, even after he'd finished eating. Noah was distraught by the news.

Later that evening, during a basketball game on TV, Noah got up at halftime to make some popcorn. When he came back to the couch, Max began to growl at him before he'd even sat down. Noah couldn't believe it. He was instantly overwhelmed with disappointment, frustration and despair. He left the dog in the living room and went straight to bed, trying to forget about what happened.

The next day, everything seemed to be back to normal. Max woke up Noah with cuddles, and in the evening, they were back on the sofa together in peace.

Several days passed without another episode, but the following weekend, Max tried to attack a poodle during one of his walks – for no reason that Noah could see.

Months went by and the incidents continued, becoming more frequent, until one day it came to a head. Max bit Noah's friend who had come to visit. The dog wouldn't let anyone into the house anymore, and sharing the sofa with him became impossible.

MAX'S RECOVERY PROGRAM

Noah's dream of owning a 'gentle giant' Rottweiler was shattered, but he decided to take action. In order to control Max's aggression, Noah had to reassert his own dominance in the pack. In order to do this, he implemented the following training program with a dog trainer's help.

The first week of the program included some tough love. Noah had to drastically reduce all contact with Max while they were in the house. That meant no talking, petting or even looking at him. Simultaneously, he had to increase interaction with him outside the home. In addition to their normal daily walk where they'd play together, cuddle each other and have long chats, they would start having three sessions of bike rides too.

The second week was even harder. Max was denied access to the house completely. The first night wasn't easy for Noah, and he was racked with guilt. But the second night was better, as they'd gone for a bike ride, so they were both too tired to be sad. On the weekend, they visited the mountains, stayed in a cozy mountain cabin, and Max was given permission to sleep in the same room as Noah.

The third week, they began attending an obedience training course. They worked with their dog trainer, alongside many other dogs and owners. At the end of the lesson, they all met at the clubhouse for a drink before going home.

At this point, a typical week for Noah and Max looked like this:

- **Monday:** Walk
- **Tuesday:** Group lesson at the training school
- **Wednesday:** Bike ride
- **Thursday:** Group lesson at the training school
- **Friday:** Bike ride
- **Saturday and Sunday:** Free outdoor activities, and if sleeping outside the home (at a hotel or other), Max could sleep indoors.

The fourth week, their trainer introduced exercises to teach Noah how to control Max. The first exercise involved allowing visitors into their home. When guests arrived at the gate, Noah had to take Max on the leash, move him away from the front door, give him the "stay" command, then go to let his friends in. Of course, the first few times Max needed to be corrected, as he didn't keep entirely still when friends walked into the house. But with enough practice, he improved. When Noah's friends left, they needed to follow the same procedure. Noah and Max repeated the entire exercise twice that week.

The fifth week, their program was as follows:

- **Monday:** 20-minute training session at home
- **Tuesday:** group lesson at the training school
- **Wednesday:** 20-minute training session at home
- **Thursday:** group lesson at the training school
- **Friday:** Exercise with guests at home
- **Saturday:** Bike ride, and then Max is allowed to sleep indoors (in the kitchen)
- **Sunday:** Watching TV with Noah, but Max must be on his own bed instead of on the sofa

The sixth week, the maintenance portion of their program started, consisting of:

- A more reserved attitude from Noah when in the house.

- Clearly allocated areas for the dog, depending on his behavior:

  » **Good behavior:** Max can sleep in the house (in the kitchen) and sit at the foot of the sofa with Noah, while he watches TV.
  » **Hesitant behavior** (e.g., if it takes several recalls in order to put Max in his place when guests arrive): Max can sleep in the kitchen but can't sit in the living room while Noah watches TV.
  » **Bad behavior:** Max must stay outdoors for the night.

- 20 minutes of basic training exercises every day, alternating between:

  » The home
  » The garden
  » The park
  » The training school (1 hour of training here)
  » In the town center and in the mall
  » The home with guests (at the end of the training session, Max would be put in his place, his bed indoors. With Noah's permission, Max could go and sniff the guests, but immediately return to his bed afterwards.)
  » A bike ride, once a week

MAX'S HAPPY ENDING

Max is now two years old, and he's an exemplary Rottweiler. He has an incredible physique because Noah became a big fan of exercising with his furry friend. In fact, Noah ended up following a specific training program allowing Max to participate in many dog shows. Their weekends alternate between races, lounging at home and long walks in the mountains.

Not a bad life, huh?

STEP 3:
LEARNING

Patient teamwork reaps rewards for all

The Origins of 'Learning'

Stevo is in a deep sleep when he's suddenly woken up by his brothers, who are already up and about, encouraged by Mother Wolf to get out of the den.

"What is it Mom?" Stevo yawns, "I'm still so sleepy..."

"Boys, today we're going out to explore with the rest of the wolf pack," she explains patiently.

"Where are we going? And when can we eat?" Stevo asks worriedly.

"Come along – they're waiting for us. Oh, and please behave yourselves today!"

The cubs begin to stumble out of the den, chattering and asking how they should act.

"First rule: keep close to me." Mother Wolf says, "If I walk, you follow me. If I slow down, you slow down, and if I speed up, you better keep up!"

"Can we play or talk with each other?" Stevo asks, slightly concerned.

"No," Mother Wolf says sternly. "When we're out of our territory, it's important to stay focused, and united with the pack. It's dangerous out there. You can play when we stop at a safe place, or when we come home again."

The pack begins to move along, and the little ones try to keep up, staying very close to Mother Wolf.

Not even ten minutes from the den, the cubs already start misbehaving. An oddly shaped plant catches the attention of Stevo's two sisters, who break away and run over to have a look. Mother Wolf reacts immediately, blocking their path and bringing them back in line.

"I said stick close to me," she says assertively.

The pack moves at an easy pace. The Elders are always aware of their surroundings — one with his nose to the ground, another one alert to any signs of movement around them. Alpha Wolf and Brando (another Elder) take turns to lead the way. When he's not in front, he attentively watches the pack.

They arrive at a small clearing in the woods, and suddenly everyone freezes. Each wolf keeps very still for a few seconds. What was once many individuals has become one consolidated pack, completely in tune with each other.

"Why have we stopped, Mom?" Stevo asks, tilting his neck towards her. His legs are locked in place, as if he's frozen by a mysterious force.

"Brando gave the signal to stop," she whispers. "When they ask us to stand still, we listen. There might be some danger around. We need to stay cautious."

"But how long do we have to stay like this?" asks Stevo, already feeling fidgety.

"Until we get the signal that it's safe to move."

"Okay, okay..." Stevo mutters, fighting the urge to jump and bound out of place.

Alpha Wolf and Brando slowly move forward, but the others remain motionless. The two leaders creep just a few meters, then suddenly crouch down on the ground.

One by one, all the other wolves take the same position.

"Get down, boys," orders Mother Wolf. "You have to be invisible!"

The cubs look at the pack all crouching and staring at nothing. They can't help themselves – they all begin to laugh, a few of them roll over and go belly-up.

Mother Wolf's expression is definitely not amused. She utters a low growl, and the misbehaving cubs freeze, looking at her with wide eyes.

"This is not the time for games," she seethes, "there might be danger or prey ahead. If you don't get low, the whole pack will be spotted immediately, and it'll be your fault."

Stevo blushes with shame.

"So stand firm, belly to the ground, and try to breathe quietly." She deepens her own crouch, and the cubs copy her obediently.

A few tense minutes tick by. The leaders give the signal that the danger has passed and call everyone to move towards the valley. The cubs start to rise.

"Not you!" Mother Wolf says to her young, "Be still. I'll follow the others, and you all stay here in the clearing."

She walks off with the pack. The cubs stay crouched, and fear spreads over them, but this time no one even thinks of disobeying.

A few minutes later, Mother Wolf signals to them, "Run! Come here, quick, quick!"

Stevo didn't know his legs could move that fast! In a flash he covers the distance separating him from his mom, pouncing on her without even braking. He's immediately overwhelmed by all his siblings piling on top of him.

Suddenly everything seems okay again, and an immense joy spreads over the cubs as they circle Mother Wolf wildly. When they all calm down, she leads them to their final destination: a pool of crystal-clear water, where Brando and Alpha Wolf give everyone something to eat.

"I get it now, Mom!" Stevo says, not even stopping to chew, "If everyone knows exactly what to do, nothing can go wrong, and best of all – we can all get food!"

"That's right," Mother Wolf assures him, "and what happens when you misbehave?"

"Bad stuff!" Stevo shakes his head, "If you don't follow the rules, it ruins all the pack's plans, and then everyone's in danger." He chomps another mouthful of food and declares, "I want to learn all the signals and commands, Mom! I want to be the bravest and the fastest!"

What is 'Learning', and how do you apply it as a dog owner?

LEARNING PART 1: BASIC TRAINING

Learning is an important part of any creature's development. As humans, our parents are given the tough job of teaching us how to behave in society, so we don't act like barbarians when we meet the outside world.

At first, teaching toddlers to say "please", "thank you" and "good morning" can be a mission in itself. But these are the basics of interacting with others, and as they are absorbed, we move onto more complex lessons: how to stay composed at the table, or not to scream like a banshee in someone else's home. Then the more advanced training starts: don't pull your friend's hair, clean up after yourself, and tell the truth. Kids learn more and more every year, until they become fully functioning adults.

But how do dogs learn?

From puppyhood, each dog learns to act a certain way so they can get rewarded. There are four types of rewards, namely:

Food: meals and treats
Games: ball games, playful shenanigans
Prey: soft toys, ropes
Affection: petting, cuddles and enthusiasm

Every dog has their own favorite rewards, and it's important to play on these preferences to get the best results. It's also vital to alternate between different rewards, and to alternate between giving and withholding rewards.

TIPS FOR 'BASIC TRAINING'

Let's look at a practical alternating reward example:

- » Reward with treat
- » Reward with treat
- » Reward by saying "good boy" only
- » Reward with treat
- » Reward with ball or prey toy

LEARNING PART 2: STRESS AND REST

It's important to create a training pattern that offers moments of high, medium and low stimulation and/or difficulty for your dog.

Be mindful of their attention span, and try to gear up to bigger challenges by working on smaller wins first. If you want your dog to "stay" when you're in a chaotic environment (with lots of people, noise and distractions) they must learn to do it in a quiet place first.

You can increase the difficulty over time, but always balance stress with rest. After you practice in a chaotic setting, go back to working in a quiet place the next day.

TIPS FOR 'STRESS AND REST'

Let's say you want to work with your dog for twenty minutes a day. Here's a practical example of a week that incorporates stress and rest:

- **Monday:** Training at home, or in the garden
- **Tuesday:** Training at home, or in the garden
- **Wednesday:** Training in the park
- **Thursday:** Training at home, or in the garden
- **Friday:** Training in the city center, or close to a mall
- **Saturday:** Training at home, or in the garden
- **Sunday:** Training close to a bar or restaurant

The younger the dog, the more important it is for them to stick to this type of schedule.

Before you start to roll out a training regime, make sure you have your "stress and rest" plan in place. Write down precisely where you'll be doing the low-stimulus training (e.g. Lincoln Park, 4 PM on Sunday), medium-stimulus training (e.g. from home to the bakery at 8 AM on Monday), and high-stimulus training (e.g. outside the city center at 2 PM on Tuesday).

LEARNING PART 3: WORKING WITH THE LEASH

Dogs pull on the leash. They love doing it, and they can't help themselves. If there's no leash, they don't pull, so it's either the leash's fault, or the human's fault – at least, that's how your dog sees it!

TIPS FOR 'WORKING WITH THE LEASH'

Always remember to respect the 'Stress and Rest' concept, it's our secret to success here.

Let's look at a practical leash exercise:

- Use a long enough leash, 1.5m / 5ft at least. Once you've decided on your training location, begin by walking in a straight line.

- As soon as you feel your dog putting tension on the leash, immediately turn around and start walking in the opposite direction. You have to surprise your dog, so be really fast — even faster than you think. We call this exercise "back and forth".

- Your dog might find it hard to follow you the first few times, but just keep walking. After a few seconds, they'll reach you and go past you, once again taking the lead.

- When your dog pulls on the leash again, repeat the process, turning around very quickly, and walking in the opposite direction.

- Repeat this five times. Feel free to explain to passers-by that you have a strange illness causing this back-and-forth reaction.

- Go back and walk in the original direction. This time, if your dog pulls on the leash, stop immediately. Only walk again when the leash is loosened. This is called the "braking" or "statue" exercise.

- Repeat five more times, this time explaining to passers-by that it's a different illness — the first one was losing your sense of direction, and now you have memory loss, you sometimes stop and ask yourself, "Who am I? What am I doing?"

- Repeat the "back and forth" exercise now, but this time, when the dog reaches you, give them a treat.

- Do one more "braking" or "the statue" exercise, but this time, when the dog turns to see why you're not moving, call them over and give them another treat.

- Return home, satisfied.

Leash exercise recap:

> » Five "back and forth" exercises
> » Five "braking" or "the statue" exercises
> » One "back and forth" exercise with a treat when your dog reaches you
> » One "braking" or "the statue" exercise, with a treat when they come to you

'Learning' Case Study: Bailey Learns Boundaries

MEET BAILEY

Sophia and Liam had a great life, but they decided to fill it with even more joy. So they got a small Labrador Retriever puppy who, after countless debates, they named Bailey. If you've ever brought a Labrador home, you know exactly how much delight little Bailey brought to the family!

The couple lived in a house with a garden — Sophia worked half days, and Liam often worked from home, as he didn't always need to be present at his architectural office.

Bailey developed a sweet and affectionate character. He became a mascot for the neighborhood, as all the people and other dogs in the area became fond of him. One of Bailey's best qualities was how he could cheer up anyone with his rousing energy.

After turning one year old, Sophia and Liam began to see the first side effects of Bailey's constant enthusiasm. Bailey jumped on everyone he met, and if he saw another dog, it was impossible for his owners to avoid being dragged by the leash until he was invited to play.

Six months later, it was almost impossible for Sophia to walk Bailey on the leash – he was too strong and would drag her off her feet over and over again. The neighbors, once so fond of him, would walk in the opposite direction when they saw Bailey, trying to avoid being knocked over by his "love".

For Liam and Sophia, it was emotionally difficult to handle this situation. Most of the time, Bailey was a really good dog. He'd left the garden intact, and when at home, he slept most of the time. They didn't know how to fix the issue, because Bailey wasn't intentionally misbehaving - he was just trying to play.

BAILEY'S RECOVERY PROGRAM

After turning two, Bailey had grown so strong that he could even over-power Liam. The couple finally decided to follow a recovery program.

In the first week, Bailey's hyperactivity needed to be controlled. He could be subdued by challenging his relationship with the most important thing for most dogs: food. His sense of smell is highly developed (like all dogs, but some Labradors are truly incredible) so his attention was captured as soon as he smelled his lunch.

The couple began to feed Bailey in various ways in the first week:

- **Monday:** He got his daily ration during a 20-minute exercise learning "sit" and "down".

- **Tuesday:** Dry food was placed into a 'snack ball', so Bailey had to push and roll the ball around to get the food out. This was done piece by piece.

- **Wednesday:** Liam scattered dry food over a section in the garden, so Bailey had to find each individual piece among the grass and plants.

- **Thursday:** Liam held onto Bailey, while Sophia hid the bowl. She might put it in the bathroom, behind a tree in the garden, under the car, or elsewhere. Then Bailey was released and had to seek out his meal.

- **Friday:** He got his daily ration during a 20-minute exercise learning "sit" and "down".

- **Saturday or Sunday:** On one day of the weekend, Bailey got his food outside the home, in the park or countryside. Liam kept Bailey on a leash, while Sophia hid the food 100m away. She then hid herself behind a tree, or bush, or in the car. Liam and Bailey then moved towards the food, but respecting these rules:

» Whenever the dog pulled Liam, and the leash was taut, Liam stopped. He'd wait for the leash to be loose before walking again. (The leash should be around 2m / 6ft 6in long in this instance.)
» If Bailey had his nose to the ground, Liam followed, but if the dog raised his head to try and look for the food, Liam slowed down immediately.
» When they found Sophia, only Bailey could eat from the bowl. Liam would have to settle for a kiss!

For the second week, Bailey's feeding pattern continued as in week one, and included the following exercises:

• 'Working with the Leash' exercises outside the home (as mentioned in the 'Tips for Working with the Leash' section of this chapter).

• 'Sit Next to the Owner' exercises, done:

» Before crossing the road.
» Before going to play with other dogs.
» When the owner stops to talk to someone.

• Playing the "stay" game:

» With the dog in front of them, they ask him to "sit" and "lie down" while they hold a ball.
» As soon as Bailey lies down, Sophia or Liam would give the command "stay", turn around, walk away for three steps, and then throw the ball behind the dog. The concept that the reward comes behind him, is very important in the "stay" exercise, because he learns it's pointless to walk after his owner.
» At first Bailey was a little too excited, as the ball triggered his playfulness. But after a few days of practice, they managed to do the "sit", "down", and "stay" at a distance of 10 steps.

During the third, fourth and fifth weeks Liam and Sophia began applying the 'Stress and Rest' concept to the program:

- **Monday and Tuesday:**

  » At home, five minutes of "sit" and "down" exercises, Bailey's rewarded with part of his food, the rest is scattered in the garden.
  » "Sit", "down", and "stay" game with the ball.
  » Normal walk.

- **Wednesday and Thursday:**

  » 'Working with the Leash' exercise during their daily walk.
  » "Sit" and "down" exercises during their walk.
  » Food hidden, or put in the 'snack ball'.

- **Friday:**

  » At home, five minutes of "sit" and "down" exercises, Bailey's rewarded with part of his food, the rest is scattered in the garden.
  » "Sit", "down", and "stay" game with the ball.
  » Normal walk.

- **Saturday:**

  » Walk in the city center, practicing 'Sit Next to the Owner' exercises at each road crossing.
  » "Sit", "down", and "stay" when Liam and Sophia are sitting at the table at a restaurant or bar.
  » Food served outside the home, with Sophia hiding it 100m away.

- **Sunday:**

  » Watching TV near the sofa with Sophia and Liam.
  » Food served outside the home, with Sophia hiding it, but increasing the distance (the goal with Sunday, is to start at 200m and gradually work up to 500m).

From the sixth week they began to follow the maintenance program, consisting of:

- Always scattering Bailey's food

- One 20-minute session per week, at home, working on the basic exercises "sit", "down", and "stay"

- One 40-minute session per week, outside the home, working on the basic exercises, "sit", "down", and "stay" as well as one 'Working with the Leash' exercise

- One food-hiding session per week, increasing the distance a little bit each week:
  » 500m / 1640ft
  » 500m / 1640ft
  » 800m / 2600ft
  » 500m / 1640ft
  » 1600m / 5250ft

BAILEY'S HAPPY ENDING

Doing the food-hiding exercises had positive effects on Bailey, and on Liam and Sophia too, who found an (admittedly odd) new hobby. On weekends, they started looking for new outdoor places to train Bailey, and also had the opportunity to photograph the wonders of their country.

During the summer, they often go camping, which reignited a spark for Liam and Sophia, strengthening the relationship of the entire pack.

STEP 4:

MAKING RULES

Understanding what is allowed, and what is not

The Origin of 'Making Rules'

Stevo is 7 months old today. He's a bit agitated, a bit hungry, and he's not a huge fan of Brando, the Deputy Alpha Wolf. Brando is always keeping Stevo in check, controlling and scolding him when he plays recklessly with his siblings.

"He bit me," Stevo moans to Mother Wolf.

"I told you a thousand times not to play so rough. You hurt your brothers and sisters — I know, because I've heard them crying. Brando was right to bite you, so you get a taste of what it's like," Mother Wolf responds.

Stevo isn't convinced, "It's not fair — I can't play, I can't run off, and when there's food, I have to wait so long to eat!"

"If you respect the rules, you'll have a better place in the pack when you're older," Mother Wolf explains, "then you can eat sooner and explore more. But until then, you have to be good."

Stevo walks away, irritated with all this parenting. He paces around the den all morning, anxiously wondering when he'll get to eat.

Alpha Wolf is chewing on a bone, and Stevo thinks to himself, "even that would make me feel better."

So he trots up to Alpha Wolf and says, "Hey, I'm hungry! Can you give me your bone?"

Alpha Wolf doesn't even find Stevo worthy of a glance. He completely ignores the cub and continues to lick and chew his trophy.

Stevo, feeling even more agitated, approaches another pack member who's dozing in the sun, and starts to play with her tail.

"Go away!" she snaps, "I'm trying to nap."

But Stevo keeps playing, and in turn receives two well-aimed bites.

He whimpers and darts back to his siblings, where he lies down to lick his wounds. After a few minutes of self-pity, he gathers himself up and starts playing with his brothers.

Mother Wolf watches him, feeling concerned. She knows if he continues disobeying and disrespecting the pack, he could get into serious trouble. The Alpha Wolf is patient, but she knows he's made an example of young rebels before.

Days pass, and Stevo's mood swings continue. The situation worsens after a successful hunt. The wolves begin to eat voraciously, but their hunger is controlled by respect for the rules of the pack. What may look like a messy buffet to an outsider is actually governed by a strict hierarchy. Stevo and the other youngsters know they must wait agonizing minutes before it's their turn to get close to the kill. By the time they get to the meal, all the best parts are always long gone.

But today, our favorite young wolf has no intention of settling for leftovers.

Stevo studies the scene and waits for the perfect moment to enter the feast. As his brothers and sisters hang back for their turn, Stevo marches up to Brando, who blocks his way and ignores him completely.

Out of nowhere, Stevo lets out a powerful growl.

Brando's reaction is immediate: he turns and, snarling menacingly, chases Stevo away from the kill. Stevo immediately regrets his stunt and howls in disappointment.

Now Alpha Wolf gets involved, effortlessly tossing the youngster aside, attacking him, and racing after him until Stevo is far away from the pack.

Half an hour passes, and Stevo tries to get close again. This time, the entire pack is against him, growling at first, then chasing him off as soon as he dares trying to join them. Only his mom hangs back, sadness in her eyes.

Eventually, even she turns away and joins the pack again.

This second chase lasts longer than the first, and with everyone shunning him, Stevo realizes he's completely isolated. Dejected, he decides to go to the watering hole to drink. He's sure he'll find something to eat there too.

But water is the only thing Stevo will consume for the next three days.

"I don't get it, how am I supposed to eat?" he thinks. After wandering around the watering hole, he finds nothing. He tries digging desperately hoping to find a rodent or even a grub. No luck.

He spends his first night feeling angry, but that anger slowly turns to fear as he shivers with no siblings to cuddle for warmth. The next day, rain starts to pour from the sky, and he can't find a single place to rest that isn't soaked.

Stevo wanders like a lost soul for three days, completely clueless and increasingly hungry. He's afraid. He remembers Mother Wolf's words, "without the pack, you won't survive." Those words take on a whole new meaning now, as he struggles to sleep another lonely night.

At sunrise, in the distance, he hears the excitement of his pack. "Food! They found food. What I wouldn't give for a tiny scrap. I'd do anything," he says to himself – since there's nobody else to talk to.

Driven by hunger and despair, he finds the courage to move towards what has been, up until now, the center of his universe — the wolf pack.

He sees his family in the distance, and just the thought of being bullied and chased away again makes him feel tiny. So, with his tail between his legs, he slowly approaches the pack. The others see him, but they don't move. He walks up to Alpha Wolf, stops ten meters away, and waits until the leader sees him.

Stevo finds his voice, "I'm sorry everyone. I'll never disrespect the rules again."

There's a long silence as Alpha Wolf stares him down. Then, something shifts, his face relaxes, and he turns back to the feast.

"Come," says Brando, inviting Stevo to take his place next to his siblings.

Stevo can't believe his luck as he humbly takes his spot, waiting patiently for his turn at lunch.

Once he eats, Stevo is overwhelmed with gratitude – this must be the best meal he's had in his entire life!

"For a while there, I didn't think I was ever going to eat again," he says to his sister, mouth full of food.

"We're glad you're back – even though it means one more wolf to share food with!" his sister chuckles.

"Mom," Stevo says after the meal, when everyone is lounging around and digesting, "How can you live without eating? Eating is the best thing in the world!"

"That's right, you can't live without food," Mother Wolf responds, laughing, "it took you long enough to figure that out. And more importantly, you can only have good food if the whole pack works together."

"Food's amazing, Mom!" Stevo grins, "And how awesome is this family? Who invented the pack, Mom? It feels so good to live with you all again, and to be part of the pack. I took it for granted before, but now — now I truly understand what it all means."

What is 'Making Rules' and how can you apply it as a dog owner?

Let's imagine this scenario for a second:

You're driving your normal route to work. You arrive at an intersection, and the traffic lights aren't working. At first, you feel happy, because your wait has been shortened by a few seconds. You're also a little relieved, as you're in a hurry. There are only a few other cars, and waiting for the perfect opportunity, you cross the intersection quickly. You were in control and you didn't have to wait for a light to tell you what to do: win-win!

Days go by, and no one comes to fix the traffic lights. The intersection is now in a state of constant disorder. Problems begin to arise, especially during peak hour traffic. People start to cross without looking, some drivers explode with road rage, and worst of all — some drivers become selfish, and don't consider others as they barrel through the busy intersection.

The situation starts to stress you out a little, as you need to pay very close attention every time you're at the intersection. When the traffic lights were working, you never worried about this part of your journey, perhaps only thinking about the delicious dinner that's waiting for you at home. Now you must concentrate, and you can't get distracted even for a second, in case an inexperienced driver smashes into your car! Over the next couple of days, you run the risk accidents, and you're mistreated by rude drivers too.

Your feelings begin to change:

Anxiety: before arriving at the crossing, you start worrying because you never know what you'll be faced with.

Hyperactivity: you rush, trying to speed up the process just to get it over with, and this mood stays with you long after you've left the danger zone.

Fear: the arrival of a taxi (that has no intention of stopping) forces you to brake suddenly, leaving your heart racing, and you wonder if it would've been better to take the bus today, or a taxi — that taxi!

Aggression: yes, you're a fairly calm person, but after days of getting your buttons pushed, you flip out, screaming profanities at the car in front of you – for that one moment, you want to chase that car and bite the driver's ear off!

A week into the saga, you can barely remember the relief you felt the first day the lights were out. Even though you left your home calm and collected after having a delicious breakfast, the chaos on the road is a dark spot in your morning.

In your own little way, you're becoming a bit of a psychopath. Depending on your true character, you will lean more towards fear or aggression, or both — perhaps fear makes you aggressive? You might develop more anxiety, or you could become more hyperactive throughout the day... all because of the lawless unpredictability of that one intersection.

Dogs often live in these "cities without traffic lights". Sometimes we, with all the best intentions, turn off all the traffic lights in our dog's world.

We saw in Chapter 2, "Living in a Pack," how important it is for your dog to have a leader, a guiding light to feel secure within his pack. Now, we need to realize that a lack of rules doesn't make a dog happy — it makes them stressed.

TIPS FOR 'MAKING RULES'

There are three behaviors that need to be prevented, or, if they've already happened, need to be controlled, to bring your dog back to normality. We need rules to repair and prevent these three issues:

Fear and Anxiety

These behaviors have a strong genetic basis, but our attitude and the rules we set can intensify fear or anxiety in our dogs. With the correct socialization or resocialization, (as discussed in Chapter 1, "Socialization"), we can help our furry friends greatly by re-establishing the balance they crave.

Fear is a natural feeling that keeps dogs safe in dangerous situations. However, when it becomes excessive, we have a problem. If fear overpowers the dog even when the danger has passed, or they start to show

51

signs of fear before danger even arrives, we have anxiety. This makes the dog feel completely useless and without purpose, and leaves the owner distressed as well.

Hyperactivity

If a dog isn't active enough, this can create a build-up of energy. It needs to be released somehow. If it isn't directed into constructive activities, the excess energy will show up as inappropriate behavior, like pulling the leash, jumping excessively, or destroying parts of the garden. This is the dog's way of telling us that they need more exercise, and it's our job to give them plenty of opportunities to let off steam.

Aggression

The most serious case is when the dog is aggressive towards their owner or family, trying to showcase dominance. Protective dogs may show territorial aggression, usually in the home or garden, or predatory aggression, when they attack everything that moves erratically and/or other animals. These, along with possessive aggression, are less severe issues, but can still be very dangerous if left unchecked.

Intraspecific competition happens when two animals of the same species compete for limited resources. This often occurs between dogs of the same sex, creating serious behavioral problems, but it's also of medium severity.

Other types of aggression might spring from fear, pain and maternal instincts. These are always annoying and need to be resolved with a suitable program, but are less severe than the others.

'MAKING RULES' PUT INTO PRACTICE

If we correctly take care of our dog, they'll learn to respect our simple rules. You can explain this to your pooch with these pointers:

- The walk is not a wild ride where you drag a full-grown human along! It's a relaxing time when you can calmly sniff around, investigate, and "update yourself" on the latest news in the Canine World – and I can get mesmerized by the physique of the personal trainer that runs in the park.

- People love dogs, but their clothes don't! You can't just jump on any-one who looks friendly. That's against our rules, and I won't allow it.

- Other dogs can be great fun, but you can't launch yourself at them like a rocket every time you see one! No, you can't. You'll wait, sit next to me, and if you're well behaved, only then can you go have fun with your new best friends.

- You get nice people and nice dogs, but there are also unpleasant ones out there. Some are downright hateful! But you can't attack them just because you don't like them. You're a faithful companion, and I thank you for wanting to "take out the trash," but no thanks. I'll handle it — you just watch my back!

- One pack of your dry food costs $80. Let me eat my steak, that I bought at the discount store for $2, in peace. You can't stare at me and drool on my leg every time I sit at the table. That's not cool!

- It's very thoughtful of you to follow me into the bathroom to watch me brush my teeth, but you can't always join me in every room. And I know the couch is comfy, but we can't all crowd onto it — I'm a fully-grown human and you're a Great Dane! I've set up a spot for your bed at the foot of the couch, so use it please.

- You can join me at the bar and in restaurants, but only if you're quiet, and you don't make puppy-dog eyes at the waiter.

- I'm a good driver, but when you jump on me while I'm driving, I can't keep us safe on the road. Stay in your place, or stay at home!

'Making Rules' Case Study: Jack's Home Alone

MEET JACK

When Mason and Isabella decided to get a German Shepherd puppy, they agonized over the idea that sometimes, the dog would have to be home alone, as they both led busy lives. They decided to take the plunge and bring little Jack home, determined to keep him company as much as possible so he wouldn't be lonely and stressed.

Every day, when he heard the keys rattle in the door, Jack knew his owners were home. As soon as they walked through the door, their overly panicked affection would start: "Jack! Jack, love. Mommy and Daddy are back! Here, look what we bought you! Come here, I want to give you a massive cuddle! Did you miss us? Come, I'll make you a snack! No, let's go for a walk! Mason, where did you put the leash? Can you bring it, and don't forget to bring the ball!"

At first, Jack didn't understand why there was so much fuss. "Yes," he thought, "I'm also very happy to see you two, but if you carry on like this I'm going to freak out! Sure, you left me alone for a few hours and I got a little bored — at one point I even started crying, but then I calmed down and had a nap. I knew you'd be back."

As the days passed, the little German Shepherd began to feel doubtful when his owners said their guilt-ridden goodbyes.

Jack would watch the door close and start to wonder, "why are they so scared to leave me alone? Maybe there's danger in the house?! It's the only explanation! I need to stay alert," he'd start pacing, "I hope they come back soon! Oh no, what if the danger hits me when I'm alone — maybe it's better if I call out to them with some howling? I'm so stressed! I'll dig a hole in the garden — maybe that'll calm me down...."

And of course, when Mason and Isabella came home, the garden was dug up, a few couch cushions destroyed, and the neighbors had left a message that Jack's howling was getting on their nerves!

Poor Jack wasn't trying to misbehave or cause trouble. This is a prime example of separation anxiety.

It's perfectly natural to shower a puppy with affection and attention when they arrive at their new home. It's important that a new dog feels welcome and the owners are emotionally available and engaged with their pooch. But what Mason and Isabella didn't understand is there are other ways to keep a dog happy and peaceful, even when you must leave them home alone.

Jack had seemed like an independent puppy at first, but quickly began to follow them everywhere around the house. Sometimes when one of them walked away, even for a second, he would have a mini panic attack.

Whenever they both left the house, Mason and Isabella would return to some fresh damage done to the garden. Their neighbors kept complaining about Jack's constant howling, which stopped as soon as one of them came home. It felt like little Jack couldn't breathe unless they were there with him.

Fortunately, the couple soon realized there was a problem, and took the situation in hand.

JACK'S RECOVERY PROGRAM

Jack's recovery program was followed precisely for forty days, but first, it was important that Mason and Isabella understood that love and obsession were two completely different feelings. Love is warm and gentle. Obsession is sharp, suffocating, and can even burn us with its unbearable heat.

Jack's clingy attitude didn't stem from love, but rather insecurity that led to an obsession with being around his owners. Therefore, they didn't need to feel guilty for correcting his behavior. In fact, it was an act of love to help Jack overcome his obsession.

Three sessions were dedicated to understanding this concept. After these fundamentals were covered, Isabella and Mason were ready to help their furry friend learn to stay calm when they weren't around.

- Isabella and Mason began by simulating their departure:

  » They'd prepare to leave, but then would sit down to have a coffee.
  » They'd go out for a few minutes, then come back into the house without even looking at the dog.
  » They'd watch TV close to bedtime, in their pajamas, then leave the house quickly, and immediately come back inside.

- They also increased the length of morning walks. They would take turns getting up half an hour earlier to take Jack for a nice long walk.

- Twenty minutes before leaving the house, they'd start to act detached from the dog, not looking at him or speaking to him. They had to be completely indifferent, acting very calm and quiet when they left the house, as if they'd return a minute later (like in the simulation exercises).

- They introduced new toys, given to Jack only when he was left alone. Toys that were pleasant to nibble on were best, or ones where treats could be hidden inside.

- They introduced the food scattering method in a section in the garden, so Jack took a lot longer to finish his meal. For the same reason, they would sometimes serve his food into a 'snack ball' so that he'd have to work for each piece.

- When they got home, Mason and Isabella would let Jack perform and go wild, but try and ignore him completely. This would go on for around twenty minutes, or until he would calm down and lie in his bed.

- All of Jack's overly attached behavior was discouraged (for example, when he would follow them into every room of the house) by completely ignoring him. On the other hand, he got lots of love and attention when he was quiet in his bed.

- The most important exercise was "stay in your bed". Jack was sent there regularly when he was agitated and had to stay even if they were moving between rooms. After a few weeks, "stay in your bed" was called right before the twenty minutes of ignoring they would do before leaving the dog alone.

- The reduced interaction inside the home was offset by increased interaction outside the home. The couple had to learn to be more enthusiastic when they were at the park, or during their walk, giving Jack plenty of positive attention and affection.

JACK'S HAPPY ENDING

Four months after starting this therapy, the happy family had developed the perfect balance of love and independence. Jack was still loving and playful, but he hardly seemed to notice when his owners would come and go. His destructive behavior faded away as he grew up into a peaceful, confident dog.

Their family bond was now based on the joy of each other's company, and not on need and insecurity. This revelation had the added benefit of bringing Isabella and Mason closer together too.

STEP 5:

FOLLOWING INSTINCT

Finding and embracing instinctual behavior

The Origin of 'Following Instinct'

"This time it's for real, guys," warns Brando, speaking to the boys. "We're leaving for a proper hunt, so get ready. We won't be back for a while."

Stevo is now one and a half years old. He's already been on several hunts with the pack, but he was hardly the star player, always struggling to co-ordinate with the adults. The hunters move in perfect harmony and seem to understand each other instantly. It fascinates him, and he's always focused on improving. He observes carefully, then mimics every move he sees with relish. Being a wolf makes him feel so good!

After their usual break at the watering hole, Alpha Wolf and Brando figure out the best route to take for their hunt. Stevo notices the leaders aren't sniffing around like they usually do at this point. Instead, they're strat-egizing, discussing how their prey's habits change during this season. With their years of experience, they know more than any human expert in wildlife behavior could dream of.

The leaders finally make their decision, and the hunting party get moving. The pace ramps up until they're going at a fast clip. As a cub, Stevo would've felt nothing but a dizzying blur at this speed, but his co-ordination has been improving every day. Now he hears and smells every-thing, and is slowly starting to recognize all the nuances of this world. He loves his life. He's bursting with joy, and part of him wants to jump and yelp and play with all this energy – but he knows they're on a mission, and keeps himself present and attentive.

After a few hours of venturing through the woods, the group slows down dramatically.

"We're close to the border of another pack's territory," Brando announces. "Be cautious, and stop if you feel something isn't right. If there's danger, don't be a hero, just find a place to hide."

Alpha Wolf starts to assign tasks. The expert hunters split up into two groups, advancing ahead of the pack. One group investigates the land to the right, and the other group heads left. Stevo and the other young wolves are told to stay where they are, keeping an eye on the clearing around them.

"We're all in this together," says Alpha Wolf to the youngsters, "but if you get in trouble, turn around immediately, and go back home. Stay calm and follow our tracks. If you lose the way, slow down and try to find our path by sniffing and studying everything around you."

Alpha Wolf heads off, and Stevo is filled with glee. Finally, he can release all his inhibitions! He starts to run in the clearing, but then turns to the right.

His senses are heightened — his eyes, ears, nose, and paws feed him information, and all those messages merge into an all-encompassing sense of the moment he's in.

He slows down suddenly. Under a tree ahead, Stevo gets a whiff of a strong smell. "It's a den," he thinks, "okay, I know what to do."

He slowly comes up to the tree and starts to dig. He can feel the earth becoming moist the deeper he digs. He tries to sniff around, but only picks up mud.

Suddenly, a new sense seems to be switched on, like a gentle warning sign. It tells him to stop. Suppressing his excitement, he looks around warily.

"A presence. Someone is around," this strange sensation, his intuition, whispers to him. Stevo doesn't understand why, but he trusts the voice completely. In a moment, his nose confirms the truth: a new, yet oddly familiar scent is nearby.

His eyes scan the bushes around him and suddenly, he sees her. A female wolf, a stranger, is watching him.

"Ahem," Stevo says shyly, "I can see you..." his curiosity is piqued, but he feels his body getting ready to run if this goes wrong.

The female wolf strolls out of her hiding spot. Another strange phenomenon hits Stevo, as if a powerful magnet is drawing him towards her. This urge is competing with his fear and readiness to pull back to his pack. These two forces are at odds inside him, and Stevo can't do much but stand perfectly still.

The new wolf approaches him slowly.

He can't move a muscle. In a flash, she's right in his space. He lets her smell him. He, in turn, gets a whiff of her – she smells incredible. His heart beats wildly in his chest. The female wolf now moves in a very familiar way – just like his siblings do when they want to play.

Then she turns and starts to run, and run, and run.

Stevo follows her without thinking twice. The urge pulling him back to his pack has faded away, and he follows the female single-mindedly. They run together for a long time, sometimes stopping to play. Stevo notices the way he plays is different with her. Normally he'd be quite brash, he's always loved a good fight, and loves winning even more, but now his movements are gentle and respectful. He doesn't want to be too rough and discourage her.

Stevo is no longer hungry, no longer thirsty. There is no more fatigue. Foresight? Completely gone. What about the time? He has no idea how long it's been since they started running and playing. It could be a few minutes, a few weeks. Who knows?

As the dark of night starts to fall, she looks at him and says softly, "I think you should go now."

And just like that, in a swift moment, Stevo drops back to reality. He's immediately aware of his surroundings and realizes that he's dangerously close to another pack's territory. He freezes.

The female - his female – runs away, disappearing through the trees.

He feels like he has the strength to face a thousand wolves, just to be with her for a few more moments. But now his instinct tells him to back away. At the mercy of these emotions, he decides to go back, even if he doesn't really know where 'back' is. He starts to retrace his steps and sniff his way around the dark, unfamiliar land, heading home.

Stevo has always felt love — he loves food, the land, the smell of the early morning. He loves himself and he loves his pack, his family. But now, a brand-new kind of love has overwhelmed him, and he's feeling things he's never felt before.

What is 'Following Instinct' and how do you use it as a dog owner?

Let's pretend tomorrow is your birthday. You've decided to take the day off, so you're free from work and any other commitments. Your spouse has offered to take care of all your to-dos, including taking the dog (and garbage) out, because they want you to have a wonderful day.

You can now choose how to spend your special day.

Is there something you've wanted to do for a long time, or want to experience for the first time? A relaxing day at a spa? Going fishing with friends? Maybe you want to watch sports at your local stadium, or a musical that's playing at the theater, or head out on a shopping spree? The more you think about it, the more ideas pop into your head, and you have the means to fulfil all your desires.

WHAT IS 'FOLLOWING INSTINCT'?

Our dogs are not so lucky! Usually, someone else is making decisions for them, and it isn't always easy for us to understand what our furry friends really want. We'll probably never know what they're thinking or trying to tell us, but we can certainly try.

It's vital to understand that since your dog isn't in control of most elements of their life, they'll look to you for guidance, and you will always set the tone for their day. The urge to follow your lead is in their DNA.

'FOLLOWING INSTINCT' PUT INTO PRACTICE

Why not organize a dream trip for your dog? Try find a spot, not too far from home, untouched by man, and completely surrounded by nature; a spot where you might find joy and tranquility.

Try involving your dog from the start, by including them in the preparations such as packing the backpack and organizing the supplies. Remember to pack anything that will help you survive a full day away from the fridge, your laptop, and your sofa. Get up nice and early for sunrise — that's the time all animals start their day — and just go!

The first activity will be an uninterrupted hour-long walk. Ideally, you'd have your dog off the leash, but if you're unsure, you can also use a long leash (10 meters/33 feet). After the first few moments of (understandable) excitement, you'll notice your dog start to follow you, paying attention to your every move. They'll be in unfamiliar territory, and you are their guide. Walk confidently and don't worry too much about what your dog does. It's important for them to keep an eye on you, and not vice versa.

When your dog gets distracted or starts going their own way, you'll need to motivate them to pay attention to your whereabouts. When they wander off, go hide behind a tree, and watch what they do.

As soon as your furry friend realizes you're not around, they'll seek you out. When they find you, your job is to show as much enthusiasm as you can!

Half an hour into your walk, when your dog's senses are on full blast appreciating the shapes, colors and smells around them, you can take out two of their favorite toys for an activity:

» Throw the first toy.
» When they go to fetch it, start to play with the second one, until they curiously come to see what you're doing.
» As soon as they leave the first toy, throw the second one, go retrieve the first one, and repeat the exercise.

This activity, like the previous one (where you hid behind the tree), is critical in increasing your dog's interest in you. It works because they see you're engaging with something that matters to them, without asking for their participation.

After retrieving both toys, continue your walk. If they still have some energy, try the following exercise:

» Holding a toy in your hand, ask your dog to "sit" in front of you.
» Raise your hand, as if you were about to throw the toy, and give the command "stay".
» Take a few steps back.
» Throw the toy behind the dog.
» Repeat four or five times, increasing the distance and waiting time as you go.

Once you're done, go find a comfortable place for both of you to take a break. If you're lucky, you might have a lake with a view, but be happy with whatever nature gives you. Put down your backpack and prepare lunch for you and your dog.

This should be a moment of peace and quiet, not hysterical excitement. Ask your dog to stay on the ground near you, but without invading your space. Eat together (each of you keeping to your own bowl, please!) and when your dog finishes (obviously before you) let them sit quietly in their place. Just like our ancestors did thousands of years ago, you might give them a piece of bread, or something from your lunch, except sweet dessert foods – those won't benefit anyone. Eat slowly, savoring every bite of your food. It's what real pack leaders do.

If the view is good, you can put your headphones on and play your favorite music while snuggling with your furry friend.

Once you start walking again, you'll feel like something has shifted between you and your dog. You are in sync, connected on a deeper level — one you've never felt before.

Half an hour before returning to your car, put the leash on them and try to analyze the difference in their behavior. Then, before returning home, stop at a public place like a bar or shopping center to get something for dinner.

What an amazing day you've had! Now you can enjoy a relaxing evening at home with all your modern comforts.

'Following Instinct' Case Study: Lucy Gains Confidence

MEET LUCY

Lucy, the beautiful 9-month-old Golden Retriever, was a well-behaved girl most of the time. Every morning, she waited in the garden, close to the fence, ready for her daily walk. After some words of affection from her owner Ava, Lucy began to trot joyfully down the road… until she saw a pair of strangers come around the corner.

Lucy froze, not moving an inch, until the harmless couple were a safe distance away from her and Ava. Ava blushed and tried to ignore the curious glances from them as she stood next to her terrified dog for agonizing minutes.

Ava admitted to feeling frustrated most days, sometimes not wanting to take Lucy out at all. She didn't want to relive the same embarrassing scenarios, and wanted to avoid the immense effort it took to handle the dog when she was frozen with panic.

Ava had long abandoned hope that time would help the situation, and her guilt got worse with every passing month. She thought it was her fault that poor Lucy was so afraid of strangers, but she didn't know how to fix it.

For Ava, this meant going to a mall or restaurant with Lucy was unthinkable, which made her feel even more guilty. When her friends brought their dogs along to lunch at their local café, Ava had to leave Lucy alone at home.

LUCY'S RECOVERY PROGRAM

The program designed to help Lucy began as it often does: with a focus on the dog's owner. Ava was extremely apprehensive and always worried about her dog, and that needed to change.

Firstly, mealtimes were used to stimulate Lucy's recovery.

The general rules were:

- Food was only available for twenty minutes, and after that, the bowl was taken away.

- If the dog didn't eat, then that was how it stayed (no different food or additional human food added to encourage eating.)

For Ava, this was torture! She was worried that her little girl would starve! Ava usually had to add something tasty to her food, and serve it with much fanfare and enthusiasm, to get Lucy interested in eating.

It was difficult for Ava to overcome her emotions and trust in the program, but it was the foundation for all the changes that followed. Lucy was certainly a shy dog by nature, but being treated with all that condescending concern only enhanced her anxieties. Though Ava meant no harm, her over-parenting taught Lucy to think she couldn't face the world without feeling threatened.

The second step of recovery was changing the process of their daily walk. At first, they practiced this exercise in the garden before going out on their normal route.

- Ava put the dog on a leash without looking at or speaking to her.

- Ava then proceeded in a straight line, regardless of what Lucy was doing and, above all else, regardless of what was going on around them.

- When people passed them, she had to continue at the same pace, and behave as naturally as possible.

Again, for this exercise, Ava had to work hard to let go of her own anxious behavior, to show Lucy there was nothing to worry about.

After a few weeks the first results began to show, and the emotional cleansing that Ava went through brought about even more positive change. It was time to awaken Lucy's instincts, to make her aware of her skills and natural flair.

The two went to the beach. Spring had just arrived, so the conditions were perfect: the temperature was mild, not hot enough to attract too many people. Ava and Lucy were there with fellow beach lovers, dog and human alike, who wanted to enjoy a little peace and freedom.

For the first two visits, Lucy approached the water timidly, with more curiosity than excitement. But on their third visit to the beach, luck was on their side.

A couple arrived at the beach along with four Labradors, who were running around in the water, chasing balls and generally having an amazing time. Lucy's eyes brightened. At first she barked, standing on the shore, and then she jumped into the water to join the excited bunch! The best part was when, following her new friends, she began to jump up to the couple, begging to take the ball.

Ava could not believe her eyes. Lucy took a ball from a stranger and joined in on their rowdy game! When Lucy looked over to Ava, she could see that her owner was grinning, impressed and proud, thinking, "Finally! You've let go a little!"

And that's what the exercise was all about: getting them both out of the quiet and over-structured life they were both accustomed to. Wet, breath-less, and covered in sand, they returned home knowing that something important was unlocked that day.

Ava took some time off work, and a few days later, the two of them practically moved to the magical beach. Their dog trainer accompanied them once, showing Ava how to make the most of the situation.

When Lucy wasn't playing in the ocean, they went through some train-ing exercises, especially "stay", so Lucy learned to stay away from her owner and wait patiently. Everything they learned was practiced back at the restaurant where they went for dinner, so the dog learned to be quiet during meals, while also obeying Ava's "down" command at the table.

On the third day of their vacation, Ava came with a diving suit so she could get into the water and, along with plenty of water games, she continued with re-socialization exercises (see Chapter 1, "Socialization"):

- If Ava met someone on the beach, she had to stop and talk with that person, asking Lucy to "sit" and "stay" close to her, and asking the other person not to engage with her dog.

- When they arrived at the beach, the two would practice "sit" and "stay" at a distance (10m / 33 feet) for 1 minute.

- After twenty minutes of play, Ava would sit down and begin to read the newspaper. This showed in an obvious way that she wasn't paying attention to what her dog was doing.

- For the first few minutes, Lucy stayed close to her owner, but then slowly began to explore her surroundings. If she met another dog, she'd interact with them, and even with their owners (without over-doing it of course).

One day, while Lucy was playing with a Bulldog puppy, Ava had to call several times to get her back, put the leash on, and go back to the hotel. This was the most important moment of her therapy, because it meant that Lucy had become independent, and finally had the confidence to face the world.

The last step in the recovery program was to bring these exercises into everyday life. All the hard work needed to translate into daily confidence in situations such as at the café with Ava's friends. Even here, the first few times, Ava asked the waiter not to interact with the dog. But Lucy quickly figured out that this man was carrying food, and she could enjoy some of it!

LUCY'S HAPPY ENDING

Now Lucy and Ava continue to enjoy public places, and Ava is completely de-stressed after her wonderful trip with her dog. In fact, those few days turned into a three-week adventure, hopping between cities, hotels, and of course beaches, helping Lucy become a real #DogTrotter.

STEP 6:

PHYSICAL TRAINING

Tiring the body, one paw at a time

The Origin of 'Physical Training'

The female wolf has disappeared and Stevo now has the arduous task of finding his way home. He has no idea where he is, besides being sure it's many, many miles away from his pack.

He knows he's far off because even his powerful sense of smell is giving him no clues. Nothing smells familiar, so he wanders, using only his instinct to guide him. Though everything is strange here, he's almost certain he's going in the right direction.

Stevo's stride is always changing as he makes his way through the darkness. Sometimes, when he feels unsure, he moves cautiously, almost in slow-motion. It's a relaxing pace after the tiring day he's had, but if he continues like this, it'd take him a century to get home.

As he comes to a safe-looking clearing, he's overtaken by enthusiasm. He runs at full speed, jumping over obstacles and climbing over boulders in a few agile bounds. It's fun, but he knows he can't push himself this hard the whole way – he'd run out of steam long before making it home. He slows down and decides to go at a medium pace, so he can cover plenty of distance, but still sustain his energy for a long time.

He crosses a river, goes through a forest for seemingly endless miles, over hills and through valleys... and then, finally, he starts to pick up some familiar scents. He breathes a sigh of relief – his instinct didn't let him down. All his fatigue seems to disappear when he realizes he'll be home with his pack soon.

But through his relief and happiness, it feels like something's missing. Meeting the female wolf has changed Stevo forever. He's a fully-grown adult now, and he's feeling everything an adult should feel (even though his legs feel like jelly after all the running he's done today).

"Hey, great adventurer! Where have you been? Did you lose your way chasing butterflies?" Brando welcomes him jokingly. "Come and eat something, you must be tired and hungry."

"Stevo! Finally! We were worried about you," adds his sister. "Are you okay?"

Stevo didn't expect this hero's welcome, but he soaks it up nonetheless. It somehow makes him feel even more mature, especially since Brando, one of the highest-ranking wolves in the pack, spoke to him directly.

"This feels awesome," Stevo thinks to himself, forgetting about the female wolf for a moment as he starts to gorge on food, "who knew I could be this happy?"

But there's something Stevo doesn't realize yet. Starting now, his feelings won't be so simple anymore, and his internal struggles have only just begun.

What is 'Physical Training' and how do you apply it as a dog owner?

Our four-legged friends (bar a few exceptions) are built to run, walk, jump, and in many cases, swim and climb. Besides simply making them feel good, these activities make them feel like they are living with purpose. Physical activity leaves your dog totally satisfied, comfortable and relaxed.

Modern dogs, however, get very few chances to really use their bodies, their beautiful 'animal machines', to their full potential. They'll joyfully take advantage of every opportunity, and sometimes will be completely satisfied. But more often than not, their physical needs aren't entirely met.

As humans, we also prioritize physical activity if we've chosen to live a healthy lifestyle. We'll join a gym, start playing a sport, or simply go for a run or swim close to home. There are many options available to us, and as long as we do it regularly (that's the secret, you see, consistency, not intensity) we will be our fittest and healthiest selves.

With our furry friends, it's the same. We need to create a good exercise program, allowing regular activity that will help keep their bodies (and minds) fit, healthy, and happy.

TIPS FOR 'PHYSICAL TRAINING'

The Daily Walk

The daily walk is the easiest way to get your dog to move around a bit, but it's hardly challenging enough on its own. Extending the route or increasing the pace is a good way to make it more challenging. But to tire your dog out completely, you'd have to walk for a good couple of hours, which doesn't fit into most of our schedules. For now, let's classify the daily walk as a leisurely hobby, rather than a physically demanding sport.

Socializing with Other Dogs

Playing with other dog is a great way to vent your dog's excess energy. Seek out a secure area where dogs can socialize and run leash-free. It's more natural for them, and it has the dual benefits of exercising them, and teaching them how to interact with other dogs too. This method does have limits, however. Success will depend on the character, gender and breed of your dog. Not all dogs keep the puppy temperament forever, and for some males, 'playing' might not be the first thought that crosses their mind when they see other males. On the other hand, a gentle and quiet dog might not enjoy this environment, as having boisterous dogs all over them would hardly be classed as relaxing or fun. You'll have to observe your dog closely to see if they're suited to this experience.

Running Novice

If you like to run casually, you should consider taking your dog with you on your excursions. This will naturally turn your hobby into something even more enjoyable. If you're not a jogger and the mere thought of moving faster than walking speed gives you a calf cramp, think of it this way: your dog's main purpose in life is to make your life better, and if they could speak, they'd probably sit you down and say that you're part of the animal kingdom too, and moving around makes us animals happy! So, you could think of this as a new hobby or, better yet, a new opportunity to do something together.

Running Expert

If you're a serious runner, you probably have a strict program already, with your days, hours, minutes and seconds logged on your fitness tracker app (not to mention your perfect running shoes). You go, you good thing! Running with your dog will only improve your time together exponentially.

If you have physical issues that prevent you from running, the last two suggestions could be applied to a family member or friend who'd like to get moving – your dog could be the motivation they need to start a new fitness journey!

'PHYSICAL TRAINING' PUT INTO PRACTICE

Beginner's Running Program

If physical activity for you means strolling from the shopping center to your car, or driving to the gym to walk on the treadmill for twenty minutes, then this is an opportunity to make a positive change in your life and, by extension, your dog's life too!

To start, two to four workouts per week will be great. It's very important to assess the size, age, and body condition of your dog before you get going. The following program is perfect for a three-year-old medium or large dog (for example, a Labrador), and you can adjust the program according to the needs of your dog.

Note: You may feel more comfortable securing your dog's leash to a pouch or belt along your hips, so that you have both hands free.

These are the first fifteen sessions you'll do as a beginner. After these, you'll feel your fitness improve and you can move onto an advanced training program.

- » 15min walking fast, 5min run, 10min walking fast.
- » 15min walking fast, 5min run, 10min walking fast.
- » 10min walking fast, 10min run, 10min walking fast.
- » 15min walking fast, 5min run, 10min walking fast.
- » 10min walking fast, 15min run, 5min walking fast.
- » 10min walking fast, 10min run, 10min walking fast.
- » 10min walking fast, 10min run, 10min walking fast.
- » 10min walking fast, 15min run, 5min walking fast.
- » 10min walking fast, 10min run, 10min walking fast.
- » 5min walking fast, 20min run, 5min walking fast.
- » 10min walking fast, 15min run, 5min walking fast.
- » 10min walking fast, 15min run, 5min walking fast.
- » 5min walking fast, 20min run, 5min walking fast.
- » 10min walking fast, 15min run, 5min walking fast.
- » 30min run.

The Two-Ball Game

If you have a bit of space available to you, the two-ball game is a great way to give your dog plenty of exercise without having to keep up with their boundless energy.

» Get two identical tennis balls (or similar toys).
» Throw ball number one, and when the dog catches it, start to play with ball number two (you can throw it in the air, bounce it, etc.)
» Don't invite your dog to join in on the fun. Rather wait for them, intrigued by your weird behavior, to come to you.
» After looking at you with a very confused expression, they'll probably drop ball number one and leave it (the first few times this may take several minutes – keep playing!)
» When they've left ball number one, immediately throw ball number 2.
» As they run to retrieve this new exciting toy, take ball number one and start playing alone again.
» You could probably keep doing this forever!

Agility Courses

Some dogs take very well to agility and adventure sports, such as climbing, jumping, running through tunnel passages and such. But before you undertake these activities, you should seek guidance from a professional. They can put strain on your dog's body, and if done haphazardly, may bring more harm than good.

You can probably find an agility camp near your home, and for a small registration fee, you'll have access to an array of fun activities for you and your furry friend.

Often, in the world of dog agility training, some people get carried away by the thrill of competitions. Whether you're doing it casually, or it becomes your passion and you start going every weekend, remember: you're there to have fun! If the stress of competitions overwhelms you and it stops being fun, you're better off back on your couch (along with your dog).

Watersports

Not all dogs love water, but those that do will relish any chance to get wet. Even running along the shoreline or crossing a shallow stream makes them totally ecstatic. A muddy puddle is fine too – those with a Labrador or Golden Retriever will know this very well!

We know that for humans, swimming is much gentler on the joints than running. Similarly, for dogs who are quite young (less than 18 months old) or not so young (over eight years old), swimming is a highly recommended form of exercise.

When introducing your dog to water, it's important not to force them, and to choose places that are easy to get in and out of. To avoid scaring your dog, the first few times you may want to avoid the ocean with its crashing waves and opt for small rivers, a lake or even a pool. There are no training schedules for this sport – like with agility training, just have fun.

Not all seasons are ideal for swimming, and if you live in a desert you might have some logistical issues, but if all goes well, more and more adventure parks specifically designed for dogs will start to pop up all around the world, with plenty of water features to explore.

Other Dog-related Sports

Besides agility training, there are several other canine sports that are designed to engage a dog's athletic abilities. Mondioring, disc dog, sledding and skijoring are just a few worth mentioning.

Do some research into each sport and see what's available in your area. Once again, we hope there will be more adventure parks designed for dogs with more of these sports on offer.

Cycling

To many people asking about physical activity programs for dogs, we recommend cycling. We often get a call several days later, with the human baffled, telling us that no matter how hard he tries, he can't keep the dog on the bike! So, for clarity's sake: you will be cycling, and your dog will be walking alongside you on the leash.

When we say, "you'll be cycling", of course we're being optimistic, as you may find yourself under the bike instead! As you can imagine, this can be a risky activity if you don't have total control of your furry friend.

To get you started safely, we recommend the following:

- For the first couple of outings, go for a walk, keeping your dog on the leash on your left side, and the bike on your right.

- When you feel like your dog is a little more used to the idea of the bike, spend another couple of sessions walking with the dog on your left, and the bike on your left too, so the bike is between you and the dog. This way your dog is in direct contact with the bike and will begin studying how it works. For example, if they want to sniff the spinning spokes and get their nose too close: ouch! Lesson learned. At the same time, you'll study their reactions. Since your feet are firmly on the ground, the odds of an accident are much lower. In turn, the bike might study your reactions and the dog's behavior (but this only happens with really smart bikes!)

- If you've taken enough time to do all these test exercises, when the day arrives that you actually climb onto the bike, things should go smoothly.

- Unlike runners, cyclists can reach speeds that aren't suitable for all breeds, so be sure that your athletic training program is best for your four-legged friend.

- We recommend two to three workouts per week, following this program:

  - » 10min normal trot.
  - » 15min normal trot.
  - » 10min normal trot.
  - » 20min normal trot.
  - » 15min normal trot.
  - » 25min normal trot.
  - » 20min normal trot.
  - » 30min normal trot.
  - » 25min normal trot.
  - » 35min normal trot.
  - » 30min normal trot.

- » 40min normal trot.
- » 20min slow trot, with a 1min fast trot every 5min.
- » 10min slow trot, 5min fast trot, 5min slow trot.
- » 30min slow trot.

Alternate the last three sessions going forward (for example, Session 13 every Monday, Session 14 every Wednesday, and Session 15 every Friday.)

'Physical Training' Case Study: Molly's Great Escape

MEET MOLLY

Mason arrived at the umpteenth tree, posting yet another flyer near the dog park. He stopped for a moment and looked at the pile of papers in his hand, all bearing his dog Molly's sweet face on them. A mix of sadness and anger rushed through him. This was the third time she had run away, and he found himself, yet again, hanging up the appeal: "LOST DOG: Molly, Beagle, 9 months old, wearing red collar. If you see her, please call 555-0199".

This time, Molly had escaped from the leash-free section of the dog park. She'd (cleverly, he had to admit) pushed through the gate, racing away and completely ignoring Mason's calls for her to come back. He'd spent two hours running around wildly, desperately seeking Molly, asking passers-by if they'd seen her, and randomly trying to guess which way she could have gone.

Exhausted but still hanging posters, Mason got a call: someone had spotted Molly at the town square not too far from the park, wandering around the organic market.

Mason immediately jogged towards the square, the hope of finding her gave him a new wave of energy. He went there every week to buy fish, and promised himself that if he found her, he'd buy her a special treat from the restaurant nearby to recover from the stress.

Once at the market, Mason began desperately interrogating anyone who seemed kind enough to care about a missing dog. A few people had seen her trotting around the market, but no one knew where she was now. A couple of guys eating chips gave him a good clue: they'd seen Molly playing with a Dalmatian that lived a block away from the market.

Mason walked in the direction the chip-eating duo had pointed, and arrived at the building, asking the concierge if he knew the Dalmatian and where it could be. The concierge gestured towards a bar across the street, where the Dalmatian and its owner were sitting at a table – and there was Molly! She was wandering between the tables, occasionally looking up at the diners and hoping her face was cute enough to earn a sample from their plates.

Thanking the concierge, Mason tried to stay calm as he crossed the street. When he arrived on the sidewalk, however, Molly trotted up to him and greeted him happily, as if nothing had gone wrong. Mason quickly attached the leash to her collar and flopped down at the table next to the Dalmatian, overwhelmed with relief.

In those few minutes, a rush of thoughts ran through his mind:

- Thank you, God, for hearing my prayers, I'm the happiest man alive!

- Molly, you are the most beautiful thing in the universe. I'm going to order a steak and share it with you.

- This was a terrible experience. I almost gave up. I don't understand why she acts like this. It's so frustrating. Molly, why don't you love me?

- She's such an ungrateful dog. She gets all this love and affection and she still puts me through hell. Where did I go wrong? What's wrong with her? Look at that Dalmatian – so quiet and peaceful next to his owner. Why can't Molly be like that?

- Today I'm going to call that dog trainer I met at the gym!

MOLLY'S RECOVERY PROGRAM

Mason was fascinated by the dog trainer's explanation. It was quite simple, really. The Beagle is a sporty and dynamic dog, bred for hunting, and those instincts to track, investigate and explore new terrain were still well rooted in Molly. Even though humans see these instinctual behaviors as annoying and nonsensical, for dogs they are a perfectly natural way to vent energy.

To Mason, Molly's constant escapes seemed to be a naughty habit at best, and the sign of a criminal mind at worst. But to Molly, it all made sense: the dog park was old news, but the powerful appeal of the smells, sights, and people beyond the gate, combined with the puzzle of how to escape, was an irresistible way to satisfy her instincts. Sure, she'd heard Mason calling her back, but why would she turn around? So that she could watch him sit on the bench and then take her home? Boring!

The outside world acted as a magnet for Molly, and Mason had no choice but to become an even stronger magnet, so he could attract the dog in those crucial moments.

Their training program had a few goals:

> » Improve the bond between Mason and Molly.
> » Introduce some fun activities they could do together.
> » Increase the dog's physical activity so she could feel satisfied.
> » Work on the "stay" and recall ("come") commands.

Mason enjoyed boxing, and followed a very regular exercise program that included cross-training through running, gym sessions, and stretching. He was pleasantly surprised when the dog trainer suggested he follow the same structured approach to train Molly.

Together they compiled a system which was, in principle, very similar to his boxing program:

- **Day 1:** Teach the dog to follow the bike. 10 minutes of walking with the bicycle on one side, and the dog on the other side (see point 6 in "'Physical Training' Put into Practice" in this chapter).

- **Day 2:** Play the "Two-Ball Game" at the park (see point 2 in "'Physical Training' Put into Practice" in this chapter).

- **Day 3:** Same as Day 1, but with the bike and the dog on the same side of the owner. Walk for 10 minutes (see point 6 in 'Physical Activity' Put into Practice in this chapter).

- **Day 4:** 20 minutes of basic training exercises like "Sit", and "Sit and Stay". Ask the dog to stay seated for only 10 seconds, and then throw the ball as a reward. For recall, the owner used a long leash (10 meters / 32 feet) to stay in control of the exercise. If the dog returned by herself, she'd be rewarded with food, and if she hesitated, the owner could use the leash to bring her back to him, thereby performing the exercise.

- **Day 5:** Bike day, still walking for 10 minutes.

- **Day 6:** "Two-Ball Game" at the park for 20 minutes.

- **Day 7:** Basic training exercise for 20 minutes. "Sit", and "Sit and Stay" for 10 seconds, and recall exercise.

- **Day 8:** Rest.

- **Day 9:** Bike ride, 10 minutes at normal trot.

- **Day 10:** "Two-Ball Game" at the park for 20 minutes.

- **Day 11:** Bike ride, 15 minutes at normal trot.

- **Day 12:** Basic training exercise for 20 minutes. "Sit", and "Sit and Stay" for 20 seconds (always rewarded by throwing the ball), and recall (rewarded with food). Start to teach "Down" command.

- **Day 13:** "Two-Ball Game" at the park for 20 minutes.

- **Day 14:** Bike ride, 10 minutes at normal trot.

- **Day 15:** Rest.

- **Day 16:** Basic training exercise for 20 minutes. "Sit", and "Sit and Stay" for 20 seconds (always rewarded by throwing the ball), and recall (rewarded with food). Work on "Down" command.

- **Day 17:** "Two-Ball Game" at the park for 20 minutes.

- **Day 18:** Bike ride, 20 minutes at normal trot.

- **Day 19:** Basic training exercise for 20 minutes. "Sit", and "Sit and Stay" for 20 seconds (always rewarded by throwing the ball), and recall (rewarded with food). Teach "Down".

- **Day 20:** "Two-Ball Game" at the park for 30 minutes.

- **Day 21:** Rest.

- **Day 22:** Bike ride, 15 minutes at normal trot.

- **Day 23:** Rest.

- **Day 24:** Basic training exercise for 30 minutes. "Sit", and "Sit and Stay" for 30 seconds (always rewarded by throwing the ball) and recall (rewarded with food). Teach "Down", and "Down and Stay" for 30 seconds (rewarded with food or ball).

- **Day 25:** Rest.

- **Day 26:** "Two-Ball Game" at the park for 30 minutes.

After this, the program went into maintenance mode:

- Bike ride: two workouts a week.

- Basic training: two workouts a week.

- "Two-Ball Game": once a week.

- Extra activities like trekking in the mountains, a whole day spent at the beach or nearby lake, or a long walk in the countryside: twice a month.

MOLLY'S HAPPY ENDING

Mason and Molly became fantastic together. They bonded over all their shared activities and now look like a real pair of athletes – serene and satisfied. They eat healthy food, follow the training programs with persistence and enthusiasm, sleep a lot, and have a lot of fun during their Sunday outings. Mason has improved his athletic performance, tattooed a (very small) Beagle on his back, and, thanks to Molly, is always friendly to everyone he meets. He also met a beautiful lady who loves them both.

Molly has changed in the best way and, while she still maintains her curiosity and desire to explore, she doesn't lose control anymore (and neither does her owner!) She no longer has the frenzied urge to run away, and always looks to Mason before moving.

The recall exercises helped them the most. Through positive reinforcement and plenty of rewards, Molly learned that Mason calling her was a positive thing. When Molly was off the leash and returned to Mason when he called, she not only got a prize, but was also sent to play again a few times, so she didn't associate coming to Mason with "home time": the end of her fun and freedom. Only when it was time to go did Mason put the leash on her.

These two really are a team now, and thanks to some hard work, they've built a great relationship based on sharing and a mutual respect of one another's natures.

STEP 7:

MENTAL TRAINING

Tasty brainwork to kill boredom

The Origin of 'Mental Training'

In the snowy tundra, Alpha Wolf spots something far in the distance, and he very much likes what he sees.

Brando, his accomplice, whispers to him, "looks like a good one," and nods in appreciation.

The brown speck in the distance is a caribou, an older one that's shed its antlers – all the easier for hunting.

"Actually, it's not all that special," Brando says, "Probably a hundred pounds. It's nothing compared to that one even further away," he gestures towards the tree line.

"Do you really think you could catch it with all this snow? It'd leave us behind in ten seconds." Alpha Wolf retorts.

Alpha Wolf knows that hunting is inherently risky business, and the pack has survived because he's always one hundred percent confident they can take down their prey. Hunting animals in such deep snow isn't easy either. You might catch up with it, but if you don't have the energy to fight, things can quickly go sour.

But the pack has a fool-proof hunting strategy. Alpha Wolf leads, and the female wolves follow, chasing the animal and tiring it out. Just as they catch up with the prey, Brando and the other males – with slightly more strength and vigor – come in to finish the task, as quickly and safely as possible.

Alpha Wolf and Brando wait a little longer, watching the caribou herd closely, before Brando runs off to gather the pack.

"Hmmm," ponders Alpha Wolf, "we could go after that young one… But no. Mothers can be so aggressive when protecting calves. Better safe than sorry."

Ten minutes later, Brando returns with the hunting party. As planned, he and the other males hang back while Alpha Wolf and the females chase down the prey.

A couple of quick glances at Alpha Wolf tells the attackers exactly how to arrange themselves. Usually they sneak up much closer before starting the chase, but it's impossible to blend in with the white snow. This gives the caribou herd a few seconds' advantage, as they see the wolves crossing the tundra towards them.

"Running in the snow – how exhausting! It looks so simple," thinks Mother Wolf, "but it's not easy at all!" and she rushes along, using all her strength, focused on the potential meal in front of her.

The second group of wolves is nearby, moving at a much slower pace and waiting for Brando's signal. The signal comes quickly as the old caribou's energy fades. The first group of hunters step aside to catch their breath, and the younger males close in to finish the hunt. All goes according to plan as they capture the caribou swiftly.

Thankfully today, the pack has a meal, and everyone is happy (except the caribou, of course). Although there's one other creature that doesn't look too pleased.

Lost in his thoughts and keeping to himself, Stevo is thinking about his She Wolf.

He can't make himself forget her intoxicating scent, her clear eyes, her grey-tipped ears. "What if I never see her again?" he wonders constantly, his stomach in knots. His worries aren't unfounded, as the winter forces wolves to be constantly on the move. When spring comes, she may be anywhere... or even worse, she may not even survive this unforgiving season. Only a strong and well-organized pack can make it through winter with enough food for everybody.

"She's long gone," he thinks, "there's no way we could cross paths again. That's the truth." But the more he obsesses, the more vivid her face becomes in his mind.

Stevo looks over at his sister, Mother Wolf, Brando, Alpha Wolf, and all the other members of the pack. He loves them dearly, and until a few weeks ago, he never could've imagined there would be something more important. Something that would ever make him consider leaving the pack, his family, behind.

"The pack first, always!" he scolds himself, "I should be ashamed to even be thinking these thoughts."

He was taught "pack first" his whole life. But it didn't feel completely true anymore.

"But she... she's so beautiful, so strong, but at the same time fragile... I can't let anything to happen to her!"

"Stevo, you've hardly eaten," his sister says, snapping him out of his reverie, "Winter is tough, you need your strength. Are you okay?"

"Yeah... I'm fine," he replies, half-heartedly heading to what's left of their meal.

After the feeding frenzy, the pack settles down. Some doze off, others lick themselves, or lick and cuddle others. Their favorite post-meal activity is gnawing on bones from the kill. Though their jaws are tired from the feast, this little habit releases endorphins, giving them feelings of satisfaction and well-being. The one wolf who really needs endorphins right now, however, is staring into space.

Stevo can't relax.

"Maybe I'll just lie down in the snow," he thinks moodily, but decides to have a go at what's left of the carcass. "Food gives me energy, and to protect She Wolf I'll need plenty of it," he realizes. Now he chomps at every little morsel with joy, as if each of those tiny pieces are bringing him closer to her.

That small moment of reawakened hope after a time of melancholy is one of life's most beautiful experiences, even though it's hard to keep alive. Right now, Stevo is like a candle burning in the middle of a blizzard.

The long night goes slowly. Stevo is trying to deal with confusing and conflicted thoughts, slowly getting to the bottom of all his doubt. In fact, he realizes, there is no doubt. His indecisiveness was just a way to ease his conscience. But the more he thinks about it, the more inevitable his decision becomes:

"I'm leaving."

Stevo's mind is made up.

"I'm going to look for her!" He leaps up, full of energy among the sleeping pack. Glancing at them all, he feels no more guilt, only firm resolution.

"First, I must decide on the direction." He heads out into the night, "Okay, this way, towards the forest. Second, I need to keep calm! She must be far away, and I can't afford to get tired."

Stevo moves through the forest at a steady pace. He sniffs around, trying to find the faintest traces of his past rendezvous with her.

After a few hours of trekking, his first clue hits him: "Yes! I remember this stream!" His lets himself do a little leap of joy before going back to sniffing and running.

It's sunrise now, and the scent from She Wolf's pack gets stronger as the earth warms up. After all these hours and miles travelled, Stevo feels a strange sense of calm and confidence. He's never felt so determined. All the nerves and fear have fallen away, and now he knows exactly what to do.

"I'm a mature wolf. I can deal with anything. I have everything I need to carry out my mission!" Stevo tells himself over and over again.

Nothing could be truer. Stevo has become a model wolf. His biggest advantage, more so than his physical prowess, is his character. He was simply born more curious and more intelligent than others, and grew to trust his instincts every step of the way.

Stevo's focus is unshakeable – not even the tasty smell of a nearby hare distracts him from his mission. Suddenly, a new barrage of wolf scent hits him. It's the first real sign that he's closing in on them. He can tell there are seven in the pack. They're tired and disheartened. One scent stands out – it's his She Wolf!

Stevo's determination is driving him forward, but he stops for a moment to catch his breath. He doesn't know how soon he'll come upon the pack, and how they'll react to him. Anything could happen. "I have to stay calm." He tells himself, "I have to breathe – even though I feel like my heart is doing backflips! I've spent a lot of energy getting here, and I need to be completely in the moment."

He looks around for more clues, "I left..." he remembers with a pang of emotion, "They've noticed I'm gone by now. What are they thinking at home?"

Stevo may feel strange and even a little crazy for leaving, but there's something he doesn't know: it's completely normal. No one will come looking for him, because everyone knows (and perhaps already knew for some time) that Stevo is special. He needs something more than the simple routines of his pack life at home. He is brave, smart, and resourceful – he's meant to live an adventurous (and sometimes risky) life.

Stevo follows one scent for only a few minutes until he sees them. Huddled together against the cold, the small pack look just as exhausted as he predicted. Each wolf looks skinnier than the last.

"Okay, I hadn't thought about this part - how do I introduce myself?" He wonders, "I could pretend to just stumble upon them? No, that's no good..."

Stevo doubles back, retracing his steps. He remembers the hare he'd sniffed out not long ago.

"It's not much, but it's a start."

With all his senses on full tilt, he realizes there isn't just one hare, but many in this little clearing. Once he's in hunting mode, grabbing a big, meaty hare is child's play.

With the fresh kill in his mouth, he heads back to the skinny, tired pack. With all the confidence he can muster, he approaches them casually, and presents himself by laying the hare down at She Wolf's feet.

The pack barely glances at him before pouncing on the hare, devouring it in under a minute. When there's only a few scraps of fur left behind, the wolves look up at him, and long moments of intense silence pass. At first, everyone feels tense and slightly embarrassed.

She Wolf makes the first move. She beams with joy and heads towards Stevo. (Her happiness confuses the others, as the meal he brought was hardly a mouthful).

"Channy, stop!" barks an older male behind her. Stevo sizes him up – he seems to have the leadership role here, but Stevo suspects he got it by default.

She glares at the older wolf, undeterred. She turns to greet Stevo.

"What are you doing here?" she says, her eyes widening. Her voice makes him go weak at the knees (which are already wobbly after all the miles he's travelled).

"Um... well, I don't know..." Stevo stutters, "I was... uh... worried?" All his confidence and pride trickle out of him, and he blushes.

"Worried?" Channy tilts her head in confusion, "But what do you want –"

"It's okay! Follow me!" Stevo blurts out, overwhelmed with the need to do something quick before he looks like a total fool.

He turns and bolts back towards the spot area where he'd caught the hare. His She Wolf – Channy, as he'll now call her – is by his side, and the others following close behind.

"There are more," he tells her between pants of exertion.

Channy is fascinated, watching him sneak up to the clearing. She's excited for more food, but a part of her still can't believe what's happening.

The rest of the pack fall into line with Stevo's hunting style, motivated by an unseen force. In no time, everyone is catching hares in a flurry of excitement.

The pack eats in the clearing, relishing every bite. After the small but hearty meal is finished, everyone thanks Stevo, even the grizzly older male.

Everyone except Channy. She stands very still, looking at him closely as the others give their thanks. She hadn't forgotten him since their chance meeting in the forest, but she never thought she'd see the charming, clumsy and naïve wolf again. She never could've dreamed of him coming back to her like this, not just as a playmate, but as a hero.

As the pack relaxes, Stevo and Channy lie down, side by side. Her heart beats fast, and Stevo's beats even faster. After such an intense day, they need to rest. They fall into a deep, restful sleep together, which Stevo has not had for a very long time.

What is 'Mental Training' and how do you use it as a dog owner?

In Chapter 3, "Learning", we saw how important it is for our furry friend to learn their role in the pack, how to follow commands, and how to co-ordinate with others. Stevo the wolf has learned to grasp the fundamentals: when to stay still, when to speed up, when to act, and when to hide.

As the wolf's lessons happen in the wild, your dog is in their own class-room, doing basic training exercises like "sit", "stay", "down", and "come back". Though training in the park is less dramatic than learning how to hunt caribou, dogs get valuable mental stimulation every time they must make an effort to understand what we want.

The biggest difference between domestic dog training and a wild animal's learning process is, of course, treats! When we teach commands, we're helping and guiding our furry friends along the way, rewarding them with toys or snacks when they get things right.

In nature, animals must solve problems on their own, by mimicking or trial and error, with no helpful hints from up above. Even with the simplest puzzles of everyday life, the wild animal will expend much more mental effort.

TIPS FOR 'MENTAL TRAINING'

Mental training is not just a means to an end. Our goal is not only to teach certain behaviors, but to activate all the mental processes your dog uses when they're alone with a problem.

In guided learning, we need to mirror solo problem-solving to get the best results. Take a look at these two experiences from your dog's point of view.

Guided Learning

> » My owner has a ball in his hand. I want that ball!
> » He tells me to "sit" and raises his arm with the ball.

» I've got to keep my eyes on the ball, so I arch my neck as he lifts it up. This position feels uncomfortable, so I sit down to see the ball better without straining.

» As soon as I sit, my owner throws the ball! What a lucky break!

» This same process happens over and over. After a few repetitions, I'm starting to suspect* that when I sit down, that funny guy throws the ball for me.

*This is where we have mental activation, and learning takes place.

» Next time he says "sit", I'm going to sit down as soon as I can, so I can have fun by chasing the ball.

Solo Problem-Solving

» I saw my owner put my favorite ball in the cabinet earlier. I know the ball – the only thing I've ever wanted! – is in there.

» But the cabinet is closed. To get the ball, I must open it.

» I'll try whatever I can think of to open it. Pushing with my nose? Still closed. Scratching at the door? Still closed. Barking at it? Definitely closed. Biting at the handle? Yes, it's open and the ball is mine!

» Next time I want the ball, I won't need to try anything else, I know that biting the handle will open the cabinet. I'm a genius!

As you can see, in both these scenarios, our furry friend is motivated by a reward, and applies their mental powers to access the reward in a predictable way.

In nature, food is the main driver for mental activation, so that's where we'll start looking for some simple tricks to stimulate our dog's mind.

We hardly need to tell you that food, for both humans and dogs, is satisfying. Think of your favorite dish – for simplicity's sake, let's say it's spaghetti with marinara sauce.

Now, let's imagine this scenario: you've been hungry for over an hour, so you rush to get home. You open the door and see that your partner has prepared your spaghetti with marinara sauce for dinner. You rush to the table (or the couch in front of the TV), gobble it down, and in a flash your plate is empty. Sure, you're not hungry anymore... but you feel like something is missing. A few minutes later, you find yourself opening the fridge in search of cake, or a piece of cheese. You might even make yourself a sandwich. You're physically full, but somehow you feel incomplete.

Now let's consider the Zen or mindful version of your favorite dinner. Imagine coming home (with the same hunger, totally craving spaghetti with marinara sauce) but this time, there is no dish waiting for you. Maybe you're single, or your partner has already melted into the couch.

You open the fridge, take out a few tomatoes, and an onion. You pour olive oil into your favorite pan, flick on the stovetop, and enjoy the oil's golden sheen as it heats up. You begin to cut the juicy tomatoes, they smell fresh and summery. You cry a little when you cut the crisp white onions, but you wipe those tears away and toss everything into the pan. Your ears are exhilarated by the sizzle of the ingredients, and the kitchen fills with the lovely, comforting scent of marinara coming together.

You pour water into a tall pot to boil, toss a generous heap of salt into it, and fetch your spaghetti from the pantry. The kitchen is warm from the steam rising from the pot as you carefully put the pasta into the boiling water. You check it to make sure it is cooked perfectly al dente*, and in an instant, your pasta is drained and plunged into your sauce.

*Our Italian co-author would like to specify that this means cooking pasta for no more than 9 minutes!

The meeting between the pasta and the sauce is like the sun setting into the sea, diving into beautiful warm shades of red and orange. You head to the little basil plant on the windowsill, pick only a few leaves, and place them gently on top of your dish.

You sit down at the table and enjoy this golden moment. As you eat, the simple tastes and rich textures create the perfect harmony in your mouth, and you enjoy every bite as if it was your first.

After the first few indulgent bites, a smile appears on your face. You're proud of your cooking skills, proud that you resisted an easy fast-food dinner, and proud of the energy you spent on this simple masterpiece. You feel complete.

At this point we should take a break, because you (and to be honest, us too) are probably in the mood to do a little Zen cooking.

*

Okay, welcome back!

It's safe to assume that animals in nature don't fantasize quite so romantically about food. However, much like our ritual of cooking makes our meal more satisfying, our dog's ancestral drive to acquire food is a kind of ritual in itself.

Your dog's predatory ancestors have quite the to-do list to conquer before eating. Let's look at Stevo's pack: they must organize themselves, know the lay of the land, strategize their attack, sniff out tracks, find their prey, chase it (much easier said than done), capture it, and then convince it to become the dish of the day – a dish that will be very difficult to chew.

For these animals, every meal requires hours of preparation, problem-solving, and coordination.

Meanwhile, the average pet dog gets food poured into a bowl, and the bowl set on the ground. Can you believe this intense and meaningful ritual is reduced to treating our dogs like furry vacuum cleaners?

It's no surprise then, after a few seconds of chomping, our pooch gazes up and gives us a look that asks, "Is that all?"

So, what can we do to make our dog feel a little happier, and more satisfied, with each meal?

'MENTAL TRAINING' PUT INTO PRACTICE

The core idea here is to make your dog's food 'come alive', and not be so easy to reach. These methods will enrich the feeding experience and activate your dog's natural instincts.

Spreading Food

This method may be difficult to understand at first, but in practice it gives the most consistent positive results. It's been proven to reduce hyperactivity and other behavioral issues.

It's tricky for us 'sophisticated' humans to think of food without the associated tools: in our case, plates and cutlery; in our furry friend's case, the old faithful bowl. But for aggressive dogs, food concentrated in one place can increase their aggression even more, day by day.

Food spreading is simple: instead of serving it up in a bowl, spread your dog's food on the ground. Spread it in a small area at first and work your way up to a larger surface area. (Of course, this method is best for dry food.) Once your dog is past the initial confusion, they'll begin to look for the food, one piece at a time, sniffing and chomping merrily on each piece they discover. You'll notice they take much longer to finish their entire meal.

Of course, this method can be inconvenient – but if you looked at a dog who's eaten a meal this way, you'd instantly see the difference. The dog is much calmer, happier, and will close their little eyes just like you would after a big, satisfying meal.

If you're worried this might teach your dog to eat anything they find on the ground, we guarantee it won't make a difference – dogs will always hoover up food within reach, even when they're raised to eat from a bowl their entire lives!

Snack Balls and Other Puzzle Toys

There are special types of toys, like snack balls, which turn feeding or treat time into a game. You insert the food into the toy, and your dog must figure out how to access it by pushing, rolling, or shaking the toy. This has the dual benefit of slowing down their eating speed and providing plenty of mental stimulation too.

Hiding the Bowl

Simply scout your house for unexpected places to put your dog's food bowl: such as in the bath, shower, basement, under the bed, in a half-open drawer, or even outside. Of course, someone needs to hold onto your dog while you do this! Or you could close some doors, so your furry friend doesn't follow you during the all-important hiding phase. This is an easy way to introduce an element of investigation and problem-solving into mealtimes.

Clicker Training

A clicker is a small plastic object that clicks when you press it. There are a wealth of theories about clicker training which would take a whole chapter, or even a whole book, to fully explore. But for now, let's cover the basics.

Our goal is to get the dog to associate the sound of a click with a treat. Here's a simple method we use with our own dogs:

- **Exercise 1:** Clicker and Treat

    » Sit comfortably with your dog in front of you. Holding your hands apart, have the clicker in one hand, and a treat in the other, closed in a fist.

    » The dog will see two hands front of them. One with food inside, and one holding the clicker. Of course, they'll immediately smell the treat, and will try really hard to get it!

    » Don't give in yet. Wait for the dog to get tired of trying to get the treat, and check what you have in your other hand. At this point, you need to be faster than a sharpshooter.

    » As soon as they look at the other hand and start to get close to the clicker, immediately click and open the hand with the food. Your dog will gulp it down, of course.

    » Repeat this for three minutes.

After a few days, you'll notice your dog catching onto your tricks. As soon as the game begins, they'll immediately hone in on the clicker. At this point, the positive association has been made in their minds. Now it's time to stop this game and move onto the second exercise.

- **Exercise 2:** Clicker and 'Sit'

  » Standing in front of your dog, ask them to "sit".

  » As in Exercise 1, be lightning-fast with your reaction. As soon as the dog sits, press the clicker. (It's better to be too early rather than too late.

  » If this is the first time your dog is learning the 'sit' command, it's okay to help them the first few times. Hold a treat above their head and wait – after a few unsuccessful attempts to jump for it, your dog will sit to get comfortable. Remember to click immediately, and then give them their well-earned treat.

- **Exercise 3:** Clicker and 'Down'

Once your dog has mastered 'sit', move on to teaching the 'down' command. It's slightly more complex for them to grasp, so you'll have to assist a little more.

  » The first time you try this, use food to assist. Start with the 'sit' command, but instead of giving over the treat right away, let the dog smell it as you move your hand to the floor. The dog will follow your hand, and finally slide down on the ground to get their treat.

  » Now we'll follow the same method as before. Say 'down', help the dog to lie down, then click immediately when they reach the right position, simultaneously rewarding them with the treat.

  » If you're patient, it's better to give the command 'down' and simply wait for them to casually lie down, then click and offer the treat. If you're not patient, that's okay, just help them out the first few times.

Always remember the purpose is not to make the dog immediately execute a command – but rather to let them figure out how to 'make the click happen'. And since the click has a positive association, their growing eagerness to solve the puzzle will help them learn these commands on a much deeper level than simple repetition would.

'Mental Training' Case Study: Charlie Learns to Chill

MEET CHARLIE

Jacob woke up to the sound of crashing and growling. Startled, he couldn't remember where he was for a moment, but as he rubbed his eyes, he recognized the hotel room he'd arrived in the day before. He looked around for the source of the chaos: Charlie, his one-year-old English Bulldog, was chasing his own tale so energetically on the carpet that he'd knocked into the side table, sending an expensive-looking lamp tumbling to the floor.

"Good job, Charlie," Jacob mumbled as he pulled himself out of bed. The grinning Bulldog started jumping at him and yapping with all his heart.

Resolving to clean up the lamp later, Jacob looked for his slippers, and saw a ripped-up piece of one lying sadly in the doorway. He shook his head: slippers were Charlie's favorite toy, and he should've remembered to put them in the cupboard before bed.

Jacob headed to the kitchen and poured Charlie his bowl of food. As the dog inhaled his breakfast, Jacob opened the top half of the Dutch door in the kitchen to let some fresh air in as he made his coffee. Charlie was already leaping on him again before he'd even finished his cup.

"Okay, okay! We'll go for a walk, just let me shave first. We might meet some cute new friends by the lake," he said, heading to the bathroom.

Jacob shaved and wondered if this trip was a good idea. It was only their second day at this special dog-friendly resort: there was a small lake to swim in, a field with agility gear, a room designated for dog washing, and many other little things that only dog owners would appreciate. He'd hoped that Charlie would enjoy the new surroundings and get some of his energy out, but though they'd spent ages outside yesterday, Charlie's behavior this morning proved he was more hyper than ever.

Jacob was halfway through shaving when he heard a suspicious thump coming from the kitchen. His eyes widened and he ran out: just fast enough to see Charlie receding into the distance like a bullet – he'd obviously jumped high enough to clear the Dutch door like a hurdle.

"Charlie!" Jacob called, but the dog didn't even look back. Jacob wiped the shaving cream off his face with a kitchen towel and bounded out the front door with leash in hand.

Though the entire property was fenced, Jacob knew finding Charlie somewhere on the several hectares of land would be a challenge. He ran to the farmhouse, where many patrons were having breakfast with their furry friends.

Casually walking up to Maria, a woman he'd met the day before with a ridiculously obedient Retriever, he asked if, by any chance, she'd spotted Charlie.

"I'm pretty sure I saw him running towards the training camp," she said sweetly, "is everything okay?"

"Perfectly fine!" Jacob grinned, remembering that he'd only shaved half his face this morning, "Charlie's just gone on an... independent walk!"

He thanked her and walked calmly around the corner of the farmhouse. Once out of her sight, he sprinted towards the training camp. "Charlie! Charlie!" he called, with a few colorful expressions muttered into the mix, "Charlie, where are you?"

Jacob spotted the training camp, where a group of people stood and watched dogs playing. Coming closer, he saw Charlie was in the middle of the chaotic group with a Beagle, an Apricot Poodle, and a Jack Russell chasing and tumbling around with him.

"Charlie! There you are!" Jacob was so relieved he even laughed. Charlie's ears pricked up as he recognized his owner, but a second later he spotted a stick on the ground about three times his size and became very focused on picking it up. The other dogs started trying to drag it away and all owners were forgotten.

"Charlie!" Jacob now flushed with embarrassment as the group of humans looked at him, "Come here now!"

At this clear command, Charlie immediately ran in the opposite direction. The other dogs chased him, until one of the humans called "Bea! Come here, girl!" and the Beagle disengaged from the pack and trotted back to her owner. The Jack Russell, tired and needing a break, went back to the humans, too.

Charlie, seeing the trend, came happily up to Jacob. "Took you long enough!" Jacob chided as he slipped the leash onto Charlie.

The humans came up to him and the Beagle's owner smiled, "Charlie made quite an impression on our little guys! He made our training session much more interesting."

"Oh," Jacob's embarrassment deepened, and he wished the ground would swallow him up, "This was a private training session? I'm so sorry I interrupted."

The trainer and owners seemed to take it very lightly though, "Don't worry about it! If only you knew the miles I've had to run when Bea decided to go on an adventure."

"We're all in the same boat," said the Poodle's owner reassuringly.

"Thanks guys," Jacob said, feeling a little better but still sheepish, "Your dogs are all so well-behaved, I wish I could get control of Charlie like that."

He confessed, "It's like he runs on a motor with no off-switch, I honestly don't know what to do anymore."

"Here's what you do," the dog trainer said, slapping him on the back, "Come here every morning between ten and eleven."

Jacob smiled, "I can do that!"

He and the trainer exchanged numbers and he let the group get back to work. Walking back to his room with Charlie by his side, he knew he was doing the right thing. Searching the internet for solutions had only made him more confused, and he didn't think he could wait for Charlie to grow out of this endless energy phase – the slipper budget was getting ridiculous, let alone the stress of Charlie's constant escape attempts.

At 7:30 the next morning, Jacob found a message on his mobile phone from the trainer, asking him not to feed Charlie, but to bring his breakfast with him to the lesson.

CHARLIE'S RECOVERY PROGRAM

The trainer soon saw that Charlie's 'annoying' and 'random' behavior issues were down to a classic case of hyperactivity. Of course, the dog's age and personality played into this too, but huge improvements could be made with a few mental training exercises.

Jacob and Charlie's first training session started with an essential accessory: a 10-meter-long training leash. The trainer instructed Jacob to let this leash drag on the ground while the dog played and ran around, using it as a lifeline to recover Charlie if he didn't want to return when called. This taught the dog that even when he was running free, his owner was always in charge.

After letting the dog run in the field for ten minutes, the trainer began the second exercise: food spreading. The trainer took Charlie's breakfast, which he was incredibly eager for, and threw it up in the air, scattering it on the grass. After a few confused seconds, the dog began to sniff and hunt for every morsel.

Jacob learned that his dog needed mental stimulation just as much as physical exercise. Since Charlie loved food with a passion, the program involved using meals as a source of complex (both physical and mental) satisfaction.

Jacob would have to split Charlie's daily food into three parts:

- One-third would be catapulted into the sky, for Charlie to seek out.

- One-third would be used as rewards during obedience training.
- One-third would be served during clicker training.

The clicker training program gradually increased in complexity – see Clicker Training section earlier in this chapter.

- **Exercise 1:** Clicker and Treat for 3 days
- **Exercise 2:** Clicker and 'Sit' for 7 days
- **Exercise 3:** Clicker and 'Down' for 7 days

For the obedience training portion of the plan, they focused on recall. This would help undo the negative association in Charlie's mind: "When my owner calls me, it means we have to go home, and the fun is over!"

The exercise was designed to create a new positive association. Jacob would call the dog, reward him with a treat on arrival, and immediately turn his back to the dog and act disinterested in his presence.

Most importantly, Jacob had to follow this process whenever Charlie was playing freely: call him three or four times, just to reward him, then disengage and allow the dog to go back to whatever he was doing. Only the fourth or fifth recall would be to put the leash on and go home.

This turned recall into a simple break – sometimes with treats! – in Charlie's mind, motivating him to obey the command.

The first two days of obedience training involved feeding Charlie every time he obeyed the recall command. But it would hardly be practical for Jacob to have a pocket full of dog food at all times, to inspire Charlie to behave properly!

On the third day, the trainer began to eliminate the food reward from the process:

- First and second recall: rewarded with food as before.

- Third recall: Jacob kept food in his pocket but pretended to have it in his hand. When the dog arrived, Jacob would show his empty hand for a moment. Immediately after, he'd take a piece out of his pocket and reward the dog.

- Fourth recall: rewarded with food.

- Fifth recall: Jacob put the food on a nearby picnic table. When the dog arrived, Jacob would show his empty hand. Then walk over to the table, grab a piece of food, and reward the dog.

This approach slowly removed the food element while still keeping the association positive in Charlie's mind.

By their fourth lesson with the trainer, Jacob felt reborn. He was optimistic for the first time in ages, not only because Charlie's behavior was already improving, but because he, Jacob, felt in control of the situation.

On the fifth day, they tried to work without using the long leash. Everything went smoothly, but the trainer recommended using it four out of five days, for the next couple of months. The long leash would still be used occasionally after that, especially when walking in new or potentially dangerous places.

CHARLIE'S HAPPY ENDING

After six months of training, Charlie blossomed into a consistently well-behaved pooch. Jacob continued to use food spreading, clicker training, and recall exercises to give Charlie his daily meals in a mentally stimulating way.

Charlie still had plenty of energy, and was the life of the party at the dog park – but after half an hour of running around with his friends, he'd come to sit with Jacob without even being called. He also learned a few neat tricks during clicker training, and became a master of 'give paw', 'take a bow' and even 'put your toys away'.

Jacob's sense of accomplishment improved day by day. He realized that for any problem, there is a solution, as long as we aren't afraid to put in the work. He could see that his attitude and dedication could progress things dramatically – it wasn't just up to his dog to behave better!

This new awareness helped him let go of the disappointment and frustration of feeling like a bad dog owner, and return to loving his dog as completely as the first day Charlie came into his life.

STEP 8:

BONDING

Doing what best friends do

The Origin of 'Bonding'

Winter has ended, and the frosty air is giving way to the soft warm breezes of spring. This particular morning started off well, with an early hunt and a good breakfast. The pack, now led by Stevo, are all in high spirits. They know they've gotten through the worst months of the year, and now things are starting to come right. The skinny, defeatist pack Stevo met in winter are now growing stronger and more confident by the day.

Stevo still thinks of his family often, but when he looks back now, he feels more nostalgia than anxiety. Being so close to the territory where he grew up adds to the vague sense of melancholy. He knows he did the right thing, but to feel completely content he needs a fresh start.

He decides the pack needs a new territory. Their current land isn't great, and definitely contributed to their decline before he came along. There are no shelters from bad weather, the terrain is difficult to move through, navigation is tough because there are no clear landmarks, and worst of all, their water source is too far from the den.

Stevo knows he should wait for better weather to search for new land, but the main reason he keeps the decision to himself is a social one. He's still new to the pack, and he needs their complete trust to change their lives so dramatically. Though the pack likes him, there are moments where they test his patience. The older, grizzled wolf stepped down from leadership easily enough, but a young male named Lesus sometimes tried to cut ahead of Stevo during meals. He suspects Lesus might have fancied himself second in line to the Alpha spot before Stevo came along.

As the weeks pass by, with Stevo as leader, the group grows even stronger.

"I've never eaten so much in my life," Channy tells him after an especially successful hunt, "Since you showed up, we've got more food than we know what to do with!" Blushing, she adds, "If things stay this good, we could even raise some cubs... the pack hasn't had new life for some time now."

Stevo gapes and says nothing, too stunned by his good luck.

Channy looks away awkwardly and changes the subject, "So, looks like that herd was on the move. Not much in our territory nowadays, even in the middle of spring."

"Oh! I can fix that," Stevo jumps up and feels the eyes of the whole pack on him, "We need to find a new home. This little patch of rocky land is holding us back, we could be hunting twice as much in a better territory."

"Hear, hear!" cheers the pack, full of optimistic spirit. Stevo is surprised at how quickly they get on board.

"Let's go right now!" Lesus leaps up enthusiastically.

"Right now?" Stevo thinks on his feet, "No, we'll leave in a couple of days. We'll head out on another hunting trip tonight, to put on some weight, and then we'll plan every detail of our journey tomorrow."

"Okay, okay," Lesus settles down, clearly overcome with energy, "but the way we've been eating, if I put on any more weight, you'll have to roll me to the new land!"

The pack chuckles and gets back to their afternoon dozing. Stevo feels himself swelling with pride at how much the pack trusts him now. "The last time I saw a group so devoted to a single wolf, it was my old pack's Alpha Wolf," he thinks to himself, and realizes in a flash, "Oh, I'm the Alpha Wolf now! In fact," he cuddles even closer to Channy, "I might even give him a run for his money."

In the evening, though they aren't hungry, the pack executes another hunt perfectly. They eat well and start to plan for the next few days, looking to Stevo for approval every step of the way. He's not the smug new kid anymore, he's their leader now, and everyone strives to make him happy.

Of course, the only thing that really makes Stevo happy is Channy. A single glance from her makes him feel invincible. Luckily for him, she's paying more attention to him than ever – as a leader, he constantly impresses her. The only purpose in his life right now is to make sure she's well cared for.

When morning breaks, Stevo decides to send Lesus ahead of everyone, with a partner of his choice. Their mission is to go south for a couple of days, scout out the terrain, and bring back insights about which route to take. Lesus jumps at the assignment, excited to have such responsibility for the first time in his life. He quickly chooses a partner and heads into the woods, looking strong and confident.

As the pack keeps preparing for their big move, they treat Stevo with even more reverence than before. He has no idea how much his little gesture of trusting Lesus has rebuilt the team's spirit. Like a true leader, Stevo doesn't only add his own strength to the pack. He also brings out the strengths of each member, strengths didn't even know they had.

In the meantime, Stevo and Channy's relationship is becoming deeper and more intimate. They never miss a chance to cuddle and fall asleep together. Channy's scent and energy are intoxicating to Stevo, and she's just as crazy about him, too.

Lesus and his partner return, bringing back detailed news of the land ahead, which helps Stevo choose a route for their journey. After ages of planning and organizing every detail, departure day finally arrives. The excitement is palpable, which makes the first day of travel feel more like a holiday than a real mission. Luckily, this energy sticks around for a few days, carrying the pack through the first few hurdles of their journey easily.

Even when they're on the move, with Stevo's guidance, food is never far away. Every hunt is well coordinated, and the pack is working together better than ever before. Stevo makes sure to give the pack more than enough rest after long days on the move. He keeps them out of trouble and knows where not to tread.

The pack comes across many places that are better than the territory they left behind, and some are eager to set up a home right away. But Stevo wants it to be just right, so he urges the pack to continue and not settle for anything less than the best.

One day, long after setting off on their travels, they stumble across an incredible piece of land. Huge trees offer shade and shelter, a stream bubbles merrily nearby, and the ground is blooming with plants sure to attract plenty of prey.

"This is paradise!" exclaims Lesus, his eyes growing wide.

"This could work, but I'm not completely sure…." Stevo replies. He doesn't want to get excited just yet. This is a big decision that affects the health – and the very survival –of his pack.

"This looks like the perfect place," Channy says, "Fresh water, plenty of shelter, what's not to like?"

"It does look good, and I think there should be plenty for us to eat in these parts," Stevo replies. "But it's almost too good to be true. Someone might have beaten us to this place. I want to make sure there are no traces of other predators."

The pack excitedly sniffs out the area that might become their new home. The place seems like a dream to them. A sense of achievement takes over the pack, and, along with their fearless leader, they finally feel like life is good.

Stevo moves farther than anyone, investigating the very edges of the territory. He finds nothing – not a single bear track or a whiff of competing wolves. After much deliberation, Stevo lets himself smile.

"Okay everyone, this is our land now!" He announces to rising cheers, "Let's settle in for the night. Tomorrow, we start building our new home."

Channy comes over to Stevo as he watches the pack relax into a restful sleep. Her expression is brand new to him. She doesn't say a word, but they both know she isn't simply infatuated anymore. Their bond is stronger than ever.

What is 'Bonding' and how do you use it as a dog owner?

We've come to a crucial point in our journey. It's time to reflect and understand the relationship we've formed with our dog. If we've learned to follow the first seven points of this book, we'll find ourselves exploring a whole new world with our four-legged friend.

By committing to the exercises we've covered so far, your dog is primed to love life more than ever.

- **In Step #1: Socialization**, we gave our dog the opportunity to develop a proper relationship with the world around them. They learned how to relate to other dogs, people, new things, and strange noises. They were enriched with personal experiences, and thanks to our own positive attitude, they learned to live through their fears, and gained confidence.

- **In Step #2: Living in a Pack**, our dog learned to follow our lead. With our new-found calm and determination, we became a good example for them. We understood the importance of being creative, inventing new games, and keeping things interesting. We strove to make sure our reactions are always positive, and only intervened when absolutely necessary.

- **In Step #3: Learning**, we practiced being patient, consistent, and sensitive teachers. We learned never to put our furry little student under any pressure, and to help them develop confidence. Once our dog learned basic exercises, we didn't rush to increase the difficulty, rather aiming for impeccable behavior.

- **In Step 4: Making Rules**, our dog learned that making mistakes isn't the end of the world. But they also understood which rules to follow and that some limits are necessary, so they can coexist with their pack and society at large.

- **In Step #5: Following Instinct**, we studied our dog's instincts, stemming from their ancestry, breeding, and character. We went out of our way to ensure our dog is living out their passions. We accepted their natural skills and abilities, and incorporated activities that fulfil them into their lives.

- **In Step #6: Physical Training**, we understood the importance of exercise, both for us, and our furry friends. We re-examined our habits, committing to work out and play together more than before. We also made sure to satisfy our dog's need to run, chase, or swim with fun new activities like agility training.

- **In Step #7: Mental Training**, we learned to keep our dog's mind stimulated with activities, puzzles, clicker training, and games. We also understood the importance of incorporating mental activation into mealtimes to make them more satisfying.

If you've been following along with these exercises and applying the seven steps to your dog's life, well done! Now you're ready to have some fun.

TIPS FOR 'BONDING'

This part of the book is dedicated to involving your dog in things you like to do. In Chapter 10 we'll go deeper into what our dogs mean to us, but for now, let's discover a few new bonding activities.

'BONDING' PUT INTO PRACTICE

If you're already into outdoor activities like hiking, fishing, running, or swimming, it's fun and simple to involve your dog in your routine. Just doing that will have them nominating you for 'Owner of the Year'!

On the other hand, if your passion for the world of dogs is growing, you could check out these activities that focus on your furry friend:

DOG SHOWS

These competitions are limited to purebred dogs. Dog shows are widespread, and you can turn the experience into a fun weekend: a day at the competition, and another day exploring the city in which it's held.

You'll have to learn how to lead your dog in an elegant way and understand how to enhance their physical qualities. There are three types of preparation you'll have to do:

- **Static exercises:** your dog must learn to pose calmly, long enough to be examined by the judges.

- **Dynamic exercises:** your dog will need to be physically fit and have a smooth trot (see Chapter 6: Physical Training).

- **Grooming:** a healthy coat is vital to your dog's success in the show world.

Agility

This is one of the most recommended sports in this book because it combines physical activity with learning. It's open to all breeds and skill levels. Be careful, however, as this can become counterproductive if you overdo it. Dogs tend to become hyperactive if we don't balance intense activities with plenty of rest and relaxation.

Obedience

This is the mother of all disciplines. As with agility training, it's accessible to many skill levels. You'll start with straightforward exercises like leash walking, "sit", "stay", "down" and recall.

As you progress (sometimes after years of work) to higher levels, the exercises become more and more complex. For example, your dog will learn to go from "sit" to "down" and then "stand", with you giving commands 15 meters away.

In obedience competitions, the dog's abilities are judged, as well as how they interact with their owner. It's fundamental that our furry friend always shows calm desire and interest when obeying commands.

Schutzhund / IPO

This is reserved for breeds with an aptitude for defense, such as German Shepherds, Boxers and Dobermans among others. It requires complex training that includes:

- **Tracking:** searching for tracks left by a person (at beginner levels, it'll be the owner) within a few hundred meters, requiring the dog to find a personal object.

- **Obedience:** your dog's skills are tested with increasingly complex obedience exercises.

- **Protection:** this discipline builds your dog's sense of self-control. The dog needs courage to attack a volunteer who pretends to be a 'bad guy', but what's really being tested is the dog's ability to withhold attacking the volunteer when they're in a 'harmless bystander' role.

Dog Dance

This is a fun extension of obedience competitions. The dog and owner perform a choreographed set of exercises and movements set to music.

Disc Dog

This is a chance for your dog to perform various tricks with a frisbee, normally accompanied by music, and choreographed for show.

Mondioring

This is another protection sport like Schutzhund / IPO, but much more spectacular, as it is choreographed and focused on functional training rather than precision. Each trial field is always different, and your dog needs to be clear-headed in the face of new challenges.

Sheepdog Competitions

These are reserved for herding dog breeds, who follow their handler's instructions to move sheep around a field, through fences and gates, or into designated enclosures. There are varieties that involve herding geese and cows too.

For dog breeds with a predisposition for this type of work, it's a very fulfilling activity. The only disadvantage to this competition is how rare they are. As you can imagine, you won't find a sheepdog training ground around every corner.

Tracking

Searching and sniffing is one of dogs' most instinctual activities. In tracking competitions, we test our dog's ability to follow a scent left by a person several hundred meters away, (the first few levels are the same as Schutzhund training described above). Your dog is expected to follow in your footsteps, with their nose very low to the ground, finding various objects along the way.

These are just a handful of the major competitions out there. Besides the sports and competitions listed above, there are also many activities linked to the social utility of dogs such as assistance dogs, detection dogs, service dogs, and pet therapy dogs. The list goes on, and with a bit of research you can find exciting new activities to try in your area.

With the combination of our imaginations and the endless enthusiasm of dogs, there will always be new disciplines emerging. For the two of you to embark on your journey together, you'll have to see which activity will unite you to reach a common goal.

'Bonding' Case Study: Sadie Connects

MEET SADIE

Sadie the Boxer was the life of the party at the dog park. Her owner, Mia, was a regular sight in the off-leash area, and was grateful it was so big and properly fenced off. It meant Sadie, who had an unimaginable zest for life, could really vent her energy. It took several hours of play for the dog to calm down enough to head home.

After each park adventure, Sadie was very calm and relaxed. Though she would get madly excited when visitors came over, within a few minutes she'd be back in her bed next to the couch.

Their lives were fairly routine. Mia owned a laundry business, so she had enough free time to devote to Sadie. In the morning, they'd go for a walk, then Mia would leave for work. When she came home, they'd go for another long walk on the way to the park, and then of course, Sadie's play time took an hour or sometimes two.

At the park, though, Sadie's behavior sometimes embarrassed Mia. In the off-leash area, Sadie began to be a little cheeky and uncivil. She didn't pay attention to Mia at all, who would call her repeatedly – sometimes so much that she'd lose her voice – without getting any reaction. Sadie always had a positive, curious attitude, but she was only interested in whatever was in front of her. Once she went off to play, Mia's calls may as well have been coming from another planet.

Mia made a few friends at the dog park, and one day after calling Sadie in vain yet again, she had to vent, "I take care of her every day. I try to give her whatever she needs, and she – she doesn't even give me the time of day!"

Her friend Lara listened patiently, before casually suggesting they join the weekly agility training class she attended with her little Jack Russell, Tobias. Mia, after eventually wrangling Sadie away from a very interesting clump of bushes, agreed to give it a try.

The next weekend, Mia and Sadie came to visit the agility training grounds. Mia was instantly fascinated by the environment. It looked like the off-leash area of the dog park, with everyone having fun – but there was far less chaos!

Lara welcomed her before warming up with her dog Tobias. The Jack Russell was a real phenomenon, but what fascinated Mia the most about him was his attitude, and the way he seemed completely in tune with Lara, always following her commands.

The trainer who ran the class explained to Mia that she needed to do a basic training course before getting involved in the discipline. The first thing the trainer wanted to see was how Mia and Sadie interacted.

After a few simple exercises, the trainer broke some bad news: Sadie didn't seem to have a very good connection with Mia. They would have to start working on building (or rebuilding) their relationship first, before getting involved in obedience training.

SADIE'S RECOVERY PROGRAM

The first practical advice the trainer gave Mia was not to 'buy' the dog's attention in any way, using prizes like toys or food, but to only reward good behavior. Food or treats should never be used to persuade or coerce.

"It'll be tough in the beginning," the trainer said, "but it's important that Sadie doesn't see you taking cues from her or feeling apprehensive and 'needy' around her."

Mia felt skeptical, "But she's my dog, I love her! I do need her in my life."

The trainer smiled sympathetically, but reiterated her point, "You have the best intentions, but when you bribe and cling to any dog, they don't see it as love. To Sadie, those actions are weakness, and a dog won't trust a weak person, let alone consider them a leader."

Mia had to change her mind set before any progress could be made. Luckily, she was committed to making it work, and gave the program a fair shot.

Their training program began with a few guidelines to help Sadie realize her owner was now in control:

- Eliminate food, toys, and cuddles as a tool to get Sadie's attention. These rewards or reinforcements would only be given when Sadie did something positive or responded to a command.

- Continue playing with other dogs in the park. These social, physical, and recreational activities were very important to maintain a healthy, balanced life.

- Work hard on leash management. Sadie would often pull on the leash and try to break free as quickly as possible as they came to the dog park. Now Sadie would have to calm down and stop before she could go to the park to play with her friends. As soon as they arrived at the entrance, Sadie would need to be calm, "sit" and wait before Mia would release her. This would help Sadie understand that an impulsive and impatient attitude wouldn't get her anywhere (anymore!)

To help with leash management, Mia got two exercises to do every day, for at least ten minutes each:

- **Up and Down.** This involves walking with the dog on the leash (make sure the leash is not too tight). As soon as Sadie passed Mia and the leash tightened, Mia would immediately have to change direction and walk the other way. This is done without calling the dog – simply acting as if the dog isn't there, and the owner just decided to change direction.

- **Three Steps and "Sit".** During their walk, as soon as the dog began to calm down, (this usually took five minutes), Mia would take three steps and stop suddenly, commanding Sadie to "sit". Sadie would have to sit beside her, not in front of her.

For their second lesson the following week, their trainer set up what she called 'resource management'. This meant Sadie had to go through a couple of exercises before she could get her food, and at the same time, Mia would teach her the "stay" command.

"Stay," their trainer explained, "is always a difficult exercise. And in the case of Boxers," she smiled at Sadie, "it can be extremely difficult, since one of the most amazing things about this breed is their natural vitality. They don't like to sit still or wait."

Mia seemed disheartened before they'd even started. "Do we really need to learn it then?" she asked.

"Of course," the trainer responded promptly, "It gives you more control over your dog in plenty of different situations. In our case, it'll show Sadie that you decide when she gets to do things, and for how long – this way, you're in control."

"But...won't she think I'm horrible?" Mia frowned. "She already feels disconnected from me, and I don't want to completely alienate her."

"It's actually just the opposite." The trainer responded sympathetically, "It's hard for us humans to understand, but Sadie ignores your commands because she doesn't believe you can cope with the situation. We need to show her that you're capable and in control. Once you earn her trust and confidence, she'll be closer to you than ever before."

To begin, they started with a very simple exercise: Mia would ask Sadie to "sit". When Sadie sat down, she'd get a reward. Then Mia, always holding the leash in hand, would stand in front of her. Sadie, of course, would try and get up as soon as her owner moved, but the trainer explained that Mia should give the "sit" command again, using the leash to suggestively pull her down, every time Sadie would try to get up. It was important here that Mia used the leash to gain control, and never rely on food to persuade the dog.

The exercise continued as follows:

- Mia holds Sadie on the leash to the left of her, asking the dog to "sit".

- Reward her as soon as she sits.

120

- Mia stands in front of her with the leash loose, then:

  » If the dog stays still (for a maximum of ten seconds), give her a reward.
  » If she moves, the exercise would go back to the first step ("sit" with the dog on Mia's left) with no reward given.

Training continued for another five weeks. Every week, the exercises would get a little more complex, and new tasks were added for the two students:

- Clicker training to teach Sadie "down" and "down, stay".

- The Two-Ball Game was introduced as a prize, alternating with food.

- The "sit, stay" command but with the distraction of other dogs. The goal here was to do one minute with Mia ten meters away.

- Recall training with a long leash.

After weeks of hard work, Sadie and Mia were ready for their first day of agility training. Mia was excited and, for the first time, she felt calm and confident too. It was a strange new feeling for her, this sensation of having everything under control, no matter what was happening around her.

So they started.

First they learned some jumps, then the dog-walk, and over the next few days, the seesaw, tunnel, and slalom exercises. Sadie flew through each task, and Mia moved perfectly in tune with her.

Meeting her friend Lara at training soon after, Mia seemed like a new person, full of positive energy, "Sadie's whole attitude has changed," she said proudly, "And I understand her so much better now. I used to think she was happy all the time. But now I see she was just agitated, out of tune with me, following the same boring daily routine. Now she's truly happy. She looks at me with those huge eyes, eager for us to go on adventures together. I never thought we could be so close!"

SADIE'S HAPPY ENDING

Mia and Sadie have become very active members of their city's Agility Club, and they love to go to competitions with the whole team. Sadie loves every challenge, and Mia has discovered a new competitive side to herself, and an amazing workout regime too.

Fun, motivation, determination, and hard work – these two are unstoppable!

STEP 9:

WORKING THE NOSE

Hide and go smell

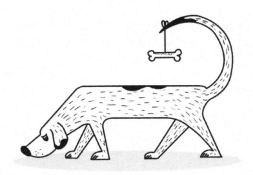

The Origin of 'Working the Nose'

It's a day like any other for Stevo's pack. They lounge around, bellies full from a big hunt the day before. The sky is grey, but it looks like the clouds have no intention of bursting.

The wind changes direction and suddenly Stevo smells a strange new odor. Is it prey? No, it can't be, as he knows every animal in these lands. The smell is strong, so whatever it is, it must be big... and somewhere near the river. Stevo rises and sniffs the air some more, and a sudden intuition stuns him.

"Where's Channy?" he asks the group.

Most of them blink and mutter sleepily that they haven't seen her. But Lesus pipes up, "I think she went to the river a while ago."

"Who with?" asks Stevo, his anxiety rising.

"She was alone." Lesus replies cautiously. He barely finishes his sentence before Stevo heads to the river, his nose in the air, following the smell that gets stronger with every step.

Stevo arrives at the riverbed and it's clear that Channy was here not long ago. He knows her scent better than anyone's. And here, it's mixed with that intense new smell, the dangerous one.

"Channy! Channy!" he calls over and over, his voice carrying for miles across the forest.

No response.

For a fleeting moment, Stevo wants to rush off and save her, but his responsible side holds him back. He returns to the pack and tells them he's going on a solo mission to find Channy.

A wave of worry washes over the pack as they hear of this new danger, and see their leader head off on his own, but nobody questions his judgement.

Lesus reassures him, "If we don't see you back within a couple of hours, I'll send a group to give you a hand."

Stevo nods and turns away. He runs back to the river, knowing the trail is getting colder every moment he waits.

On the riverbank, Stevo sniffs with his nose close the ground, investigating carefully. The scent leads him to a path of tracks, Channy's familiar pawprints in the mud, overlapping with weird ones he's never seen in the forest before.

Three pairs of long, oddly flat prints crowd around Channy's, which stop abruptly by the riverbank. She didn't try to run off, but it seemed as if she lay down. Her tracks simply stop and the three odd, two-legged creatures then seem to walk towards a spot with an even stronger scent, one that has gouged two long even trenches in the soft soil, leading into the forest.

Naturally, Stevo sees all this as a bizarre alien abduction. He has never seen humans before, let alone an off-road vehicle capable of whisking away a strong, healthy wolf like Channy with seemingly no effort. Though he can barely piece together what has happened to her, he knows he must follow that strong, odd smell (a mix of diesel, human body odor, and veterinary supplies) to find her.

He goes over the entire area again, his nose close to the ground. It must have been an hour or so since this all happened. Though they must have moved fast, he can track them easily through the forest, heading north.

Stevo sprints through the glade, completely focused on following this scent. Past the line of trees at the end of his territory, the smell lands clearly on a dirt road going through open fields. Stevo hesitates for a second, knowing how risky it is to be out in the open by himself – but the thought of Channy needing his help drives him forward and he darts across the fields.

For ten miles, Stevo runs at full speed, a grey blur across the quiet green fields. Suddenly, his nose picks up even more strange odors, and he slows down abruptly.

"I must be close," he thinks, panting steadily, "I have to save my energy now. I'll need all my strength to rescue her – and show those three creatures they chose the wrong wolf to mess with."

*

Meanwhile, at the Wildlife Study Centre, Channy sleeps peacefully on a stainless-steel table.

Thomas, one of the conservationists working here, has taken a blood sample. As he works, his colleague Sarah notes the wolf's size and weight on a chart. "She looks so healthy," Sarah says, stroking Channy's fur gently, "this pack must be eating well."

Peter, the youngest of the three researchers, approaches with a big syringe containing an identification microchip, "I've already put the code on her data sheet," he says to Sarah, "If you're done, I can take her back to the cage before she starts waking up."

"Great," says Sarah, "as soon as we have her bloodwork analyzed, she should be good to go, unless there are any problems."

"Hey," Thomas interjects, "We've got a call with the university in ten minutes – don't you two dare go off and leave me here alone!"

"It's not best for the animals to wake up here," Sarah says, "We should really be in the woods before she starts to come out from under sedation."

"Yup!" Peter agrees instantly, "Sorry Thomas, you've got to take one for the wolves –"

"For the wolves," Sarah nods, grinning.

"You know what –" Thomas starts, but an ominous ringing from the next room cuts him off.

Peter grabs the wolf, "I'm going to put her in her cage – bye!"

Thomas turns to Sarah as she flips her charts dramatically, "So many papers! This data needs to be double-checked!"

Thomas fumes at them both while the phone rings. After a few tense seconds, he stomps over and answers, "Hello, Professor!"

*

Stevo climbs on a boulder and sniffs the air. Strange smells bombard him, making his worry grow with every step. "They must be close. Their lair smells so intense, how do they stand it?"

He catches his breath and keeps moving. Following the dirt road around a narrow corner, he suddenly comes upon a barrier: cold, interwoven metal is standing between him and his mission.

Stevo stands back, judging the distance, "Could I jump this? Hmm, maybe if I got lucky – but those bits at the top look sharp. Besides, I need to get Channy out, and she might be hurt. I need to find another way in."

He follows along the fence, sniffing every inch and looking for gaps or loose soil to dig through. But the barrier is perfect, impenetrable. The smell of Channy and those weird creatures is getting stronger and stronger. The big metal contraption that left those heavy tracks is sitting perfectly still behind the fence. They're just on the other side. It's infuriating.

Stevo, usually so confident in his abilities, is overcome with emotion. If it were just himself on the line, he could dive at this challenge, but Channy matters more to him than anything in the world.

He looks back at the path, "I can't do this alone. I need my pack."

And with that simple realization, he feels hopeful again. He decides to call for backup. He angles his body towards the south, takes a deep breath, fills his lungs, and lets out a long, piercing howl.

His voice echoes through the fields and the glade beyond. Every living being in the forest stays still for that powerful moment. Though not many understand his message, they all feel his strength, and his desperate call for aid.

Inside, an important phone call is interrupted by this howl – it's so close, it gives all three researchers goosebumps.

Sarah rushes to the window, immediately followed by Thomas. Peter is in the garage just out of Stevo's sight, and after a second of feeling completely petrified, remembers the strong fence and peeks out from the door.

One glance tells him that a huge grey wolf is, in fact, just around the corner from him. That's quite enough info for Peter, who leaps back into the Center.

"Did you see that?!" Peter exclaims.

"Amazing..." Sarah says, "He must have followed our scent here."

"Definitely a male," Thomas says, his face practically pressed against the glass, "might even be the alpha male of her pack."

"Definitely alpha male," Sarah agrees, "just look at the size of him. And now he's calling reinforcements."

"What do we do?" Peter gestures with his hands, "Is he bringing the whole pack here?"

"I don't want to wait around and find out," Thomas scoffs, "how's the female doing?"

"She's almost awake," Peter says, and it's instantly confirmed by a low, wavering howl coming from the garage.

This sound sets the male bounding towards the gate, sniffing and pushing on it, trying to get in any which way.

"Stay calm guys," Sarah says, "I have an idea."

They follow her to the garage, "We open the cage here, just in front of the door. She'll come out and we'll get behind the door. Then we open the pedestrian gate and boom! Reunited couple, problem solved."

Thomas looks at the wolf, now snuffling and clumsily biting at the bars of her cage, "Do you think she's in good enough shape to make it all the way to their territory?"

Peter chimes in, "If we don't free her soon, she'll try harder and harder to break out. The sedative wears off quickly, and she's in more danger of hurting herself if we keep her locked up."

"Okay, we've got to move quick!" says Sarah decisively, "Let's get the cage in position."

Channy freezes as the strange creatures get the cage moving. She's still a little groggy, and though she heard Stevo's call was nearby, she can't think on her feet quickly enough to escape.

The three humans maneuver the cage around and get behind it. With a quick motion Peter opens the cage door and jumps back, with Sarah closing the garage door a split-second later.

Channy is confused by the noise at first, but then notices the door of her cage lazily swinging open. She pushes past it and bolts out of the garage.

Stevo's familiar bark greets her immediately. She runs to him, and he starts to bite the fence and dig at the solid ground beneath it, trying to force a gap through sheer willpower.

A few seconds later, they both hear a click to their right. A creaky door in the gate begins to swing open. They rush over to investigate and – lo and behold, it's a way through!

Channy bounds towards Stevo and they run for a few seconds before stopping to look back. In a flash, they both realize they've escaped the danger.

"Are you okay, great explorer?" Stevo asks, nuzzling her affectionately.

"I think so," Channy says, "There were these weird creatures and... I must have fallen asleep. I was stuck in some box for a while, and those creatures fussed around me. But I got out, and I feel fine now. Better than fine, I feel amazing!"

"That's great news! Let's head home," Stevo replies, "it's pretty far, but I know the way back. We can take it easy."

"When have you ever taken it easy?" Channy teases him, and he grins, running ahead of her.

As she catches up, Channy is filled with pure joy. She's escaped that strange lair with the two-legged creatures, yes, but it's Stevo that fills her with glee. As soon as she heard him, she knew it was all going to be okay. His devotion to her, his coming to rescue her, risking everything, means so much.

As they run through the fields and into the woods, Channy catches a whiff of Stevo's scent, and it smells like being safe, loved, and treasured. Something new is going to happen. She can feel it. Something great.

What is 'Working the Nose' and how do you use it as a dog owner?

In the wild, wolves and other canines rely on their noses to find food, sense danger, and communicate with their pack. During your walks with your dog, you've no doubt noticed their favorite activity is sniffing!

The olfactory sense is the most developed in our dogs. Just as we take in most of our environment through our eyes, our furry friends perceive the world as a 'smell-scape' through their noses. To our dogs, sniffing around isn't just a hobby, it's an essential way to understand the world around them.

In fact, the more your dog learns to use and trust their sense of smell, the calmer and more balanced they'll feel in everyday life.

The domesticated dog doesn't get many chances to sniff out prey, since food is plentiful, and their human family tends to communicate visually or verbally – completely unaware of the odor signals they're sending! Nevertheless, activating and challenging their sense of smell is a favorite activity among all dogs, regardless of breed.

'WORKING THE NOSE' PUT INTO PRACTICE

At first, your furry friend might not understand how to use their nose to carry out these tasks, but with a little patience and practice, you can awaken their innate drive to sniff their way through life. Here's a simple set of exercises for working the nose.

Exercise 1: The Two-Ball Game & 'Search'

- **Week One:** Get two new tennis balls and keep them in your pocket or hand for about twenty minutes. This ensures your scent is clearly on them. Then head to the park and play the Two-Ball Game throughout the week (see Chapter 6: "Physical Training" for full instructions.)

- **Week Two:** Play the Two-Ball Game, but modify it for a little more complexity.

  » Throw Ball 1 and as soon as the dog runs after it, begin to play with Ball 2.
  » When the dog drops Ball 1 and becomes interested in Ball 2, hold onto their collar while you throw Ball 2. Wait for Ball 2 to stop bouncing or rolling before you let your dog go to fetch it.
  » As they fetch Ball 2, begin playing with Ball 1, repeating the cycle over again.

- **Week Three:** Play the modified Two-Ball Game as in Week 2, but this time, while you're holding onto your dog's collar, wait another 5 seconds after the ball stops moving before you let go. As you can see, we are slowly shifting from the dog using their eyes to find the ball, to relying on their nose to find it.

- **Week Four:** We'll add another layer of complexity and anticipation this week. You'll need an assistant or be in a spot where you can tie your dog's leash to something so they can't follow you. Instead of throwing the ball, walk with it and place the ball down somewhere far off, but where your dog can still see you. Then head back to them and say "search" as you release them. As you're teaching the "search" command, say it only once, clearly and loudly.

- **Week Five:** If your dog is confidently following the search command, we can add a little more fun to this activity. Introduce a 'fake drop' when you're placing the ball down, pretending to leave it in various spots so your dog truly doesn't know where it is. You could also ask a friend to distract them, or keep yourself out of their line of vision while you place the ball for them to find. The goal of the "search" command is not to have your dog find the object with lightning speed, but rather to use their sense of smell to explore the whole area, investigating thoroughly until they find it.

Exercise 2: Hide & Seek

For this exercise, you'll need an assistant, because you're an integral part of the game, as well as the prize! Make sure you have a long leash for this exercise.

131

Here's how it works:

- Leave your dog with your assistant and walk about 100 meters away until you find a tree or something to hide behind. (We'll call this spot Hideout A.)

- Once you're hidden, your assistant lets your dog walk until they reach you. At this point, reward your dog with plenty of cuddles and enthusiasm!

- Repeat steps 1 and 2 again.

- Go back to the starting point, with your assistant holding onto the dog, and you heading to Hideout A. This time, without the dog seeing you, move a further 20 meters back to another hiding spot – Hideout B. Drag your feet on the ground to make your scent a little easier to find. Once your dog confidently heads to Hideout A (where they've already found you twice), their disappointment will immediately give way to curiosity, and they will start to sniff around to see where you've gone. Once they find you, cuddles are mandatory.

- Repeat steps 1 and 2.

- Repeat step 4, and add another hideout to your path, Hideout C. Remember to stomp and drag your feet so you leave clear clues to your whereabouts.

Exercise 3: Tracking

The last nose-work exercise is true tracking. It's highly recommended that you take your time with the previous two exercises, so your dog is ready for this one.

This is best done in a grassy and isolated area such as the countryside, forest, or in mountain terrain.

Here's how to do a basic tracking exercise:

- With your dog tied away from you, or well distracted by a friend, pick a starting point for your exercise.

- Pick a landmark or direction to follow, and walk about fifty steps, dragging your feet the whole way.

- Stop and place a (well-sealed!) container full of food or your dog's favorite toy on the ground.

- Walk back along your path, and from there, get your dog and spend about twenty minutes with them away from the path.

- Casually lead them to the starting point, as if you're taking a walk, and try your best to make it seem that you've arrived there by chance. Let them sniff and explore as normal.

- If your dog discovers your smell on the ground, follow them along the track. Stop every time they get off the track, or raise their nose up. Keep moving only when they're going in the right direction.

- Sooner or (much, much) later, you'll reach the container at the end of the track. Open it up and give your furry friend their prize, and plenty of enthusiastic praise too.

Try this exercise for several days, until your dog understands the way it works, and can follow your scent consistently.

Once they've mastered basic tracking, you can jazz up the exercise by adding new factors to increase the difficulty:

> » Increase the distance up to 100 meters.
> » Drag your feet a little less.
> » Add a slight turn to your track (10 degrees at most).
> » Make a 50-meter track, well-beaten, but add one right turn and one left turn (20 degrees).
> » 50-meter track, walking straight with almost normal steps (no stomping or dragging your feet).
> » 50-meter beaten track, well-beaten 45-degree turn, and then another 50 meters with normal steps.
> » 50-meter track with normal steps, 90-degree well-beaten turn, 50 meters with normal steps, 90-degree well-beaten turn, and then another 50 meters with normal steps.

» Replace the food or toy prize with a personal object (your gloves, hat, wallet, etc.) When the dog finds it, praise them, take the object back with plenty of enthusiasm and, after a few seconds, give them a treat.

'Working the Nose' Case Study: Maggie Lets Go

MEET MAGGIE

Emily was looking for a parking spot close to the school while trying to ignore Maggie, her white Poodle, who was whimpering with excitement in the back seat. Maggie loved seeing her two human siblings after their long school day and tried to fight the urge to jump onto the front seat for a better view.

As soon as Emily touched the indicator, Maggie's glee rose up and her whimpers became an unending stream of barks.

"Maggie! That's enough, lie down!" Emily hushed her firmly. The dog crouched on the seat for a few seconds before letting loose again: jumping onto the front seat, spinning around, and barking louder than ever. Maggie took little breaks to breathe, but that didn't stop a familiar headache rising to Emily's temples.

Emily knew the dog would get more and more hysterical until she saw the kids coming towards the car. After ten minutes of the dog yapping non-stop, and Emily trying to avoid eye contact with the other parents, Han and Georgia arrived.

"Now kids," Emily said before they even got in, "remember the rule: don't pet Maggie until she calms down a little."

"Okay!" The kids said in unison. They climbed into the back seat, and promptly forgot all rules in favor of cuddling and stroking their beloved pet.

135

Emily rubbed her temples and drove off. They had been seeing a dog behaviorist for months to deal with Maggie's anxieties. It started with the dog whining and wetting indoors, and eventually the poor thing was so afraid of being alone that she'd started nibbling her paws incessantly, until bald patches formed. The therapy helped a little, but Maggie was still incredibly anxious, and that anxiety seemed to rub off on the whole family.

At home, Maggie quickly devoted herself to her favorite hobby: following Emily around like a shadow.

Emily tried to be consistent with the dog behaviorist's instructions: whenever she noticed Maggie following her, she'd send the dog to her bed. This would start a frustrating dance, where Maggie would sneak out of bed and Emily would march her back to it. Of course, this constantly interrupted Emily's busy afternoon, making her more and more tense.

After being sent to bed three or four times, Maggie sullenly wandered off to find Han and Georgia. The kids played with her in the garden for a while, playing fetch and chasing each other. Then Maggie spotted Emily in the window and remembered her true mission: cling to Emily as much as possible!

This routine carried on until Emily's husband Alec came home. He could barely get through the door as the dog and the kids volleyed into him. He tried to remember the rules and not interact with Maggie until she calmed down, though she desperately wanted his attention.

Alec was skeptical of this rule at first, but decided to give it a try when the dog behaviorist explained the dog's attention-seeking wasn't simply because she was happy to see him, like the kids were. Instead, it was an intense mix of joy, anxiety, repressed energy, stress and hyperactivity. If he gave in and gave her cuddles, this would only reinforce and show approval of her hysterical state. Only by withholding his affection until she was calm would they get Maggie to understand that freaking out all the time wasn't necessary.

Though Alec knew the family had slowly made some progress with Maggie, he wanted to take things to the next level. That night at dinner, the subject of Maggie came up again.

"She followed me around all day today," Emily said, sighing, "I couldn't get anything done."

Alec squeezed Emily's shoulder affectionately, "Sounds like we all need a break from our routine. There's a farmhouse not too far away, a couple of hours from the city. It's a famous dog-training center and turns out, they offer weekend packages."

Emily smiled, "What kind of packages?"

"Well, next month there's a workshop on dog behavioral problems taught by a well-known dog trainer."

Emily's smile became even bigger, "You don't say?"

Alec jumped up from the table and fished a brochure out of his jacket, "Here, look! We can book the biggest villa: breakfast, lunch and dinner are included, and the place is surrounded by nature. We could go to workshops in the morning and go hiking in the woods with the kids afterwards."

"Yes! Let's go now!" Georgia and Han piped up excitedly.

"Sounds like a plan." said Emily, grinning at Alec.

MAGGIE'S RECOVERY PROGRAM

The sun was about to rise, the air was fresh, and the wet grass gave off an intense scent that seemed to relax all the dogs present.

For their first session with the trainer, Emily, Alec and Maggie joined a group of hopeful dog owners at this early morning rendezvous. The day started with a quiet walk on a winding path. The dogs, after ten minutes of curiously sniffing each other, proceeded calmly. After an hour-long walk, they came to a clearing.

The dog trainer instructed all the owners to stand next to each other about two meters away from their dogs, then tell them to "sit" and "stay". Once the dogs were seated, each owner would step back a little further – the distance depended on how trained their dog was. The beginners would step back one meter, the more experienced owners would step back three.

Alec was doing the first exercise while Emily stood on the sidelines watching. Maggie sat down on command, but as soon as Alec took a step back, she sprung up to follow him. Alec blushed and looked at the trainer, who smiled kindly and said, "Now simply put the dog back in her place."

137

Alec nodded and put Maggie back in her spot, telling her to "sit" and "stay", and stepped back again. At two meters she was okay, but at three she anxiously followed him. Alec sighed as he put Maggie back in her spot repeatedly, thinking to himself, "If this is how hard the first exercise is, maybe we're out of our depth here."

The other owners were also having trouble, but before discouragement could settle into the group, some of the dogs changed their tactics. They seemed to think "Well, if I've got to stay here, I'm going to get comfortable," and lay down on the grass.

Maggie anxiously followed Alec for a few more tries before glancing around her. Something seemed to click, and when Alec told her to "stay", she flopped down and lay there, looking halfheartedly at him as he stepped back one meter, then two, then three. Alec grinned at Emily off to the side, and she cheered him on.

This first success put the group in a good mood, and everyone was eager to try the second exercise.

Their enthusiasm was soon replaced by anxiety when they heard the instructor's words: "First, you'll give your furry friend to someone in the group they've never met. Three dogs at a time, the new handlers will walk about 500 meters into the woods there," he pointed to the tree-line at the edge of the clearing, "Don't worry, everything is fenced off here, and each dog gets a fluorescent vest with our phone number on it in case anything happens. Once your dog can't see you, their handler lets them off the leash."

"Wait!" one member of the group said worriedly, "What if they get lost?"

"No need to stress," the trainer replied, "your dog's nose is an incredible thing. Two seconds of bewilderment, four seconds to sniff around, and they'll be running back to you before you know it."

The owner looked skeptical but nodded anyway. The exercise began. Maggie got a very nice lady as her handler, but that didn't stop her from looking incredibly doubtful as she got her vest on and was led away into the woods.

Alec and Emily, with serious anxiety, watched the handlers march off. What if poor Maggie panicked and ran off? Or even worse, what if she just stayed to hang out with her handler, forgetting they ever existed?

For a few tense minutes, Alec and Emily watched the tree line, their ears straining for any sound that could be their Poodle coming nearer. After a far-off sound of paws crunching on leaves, there she was! They finally saw her, a puffy white streak coming towards them out of the woods. Maggie sprung into the open arms of her owners, whose relief and pride was overwhelming.

"Good girl, Maggie, you did it!" Alec and Emily praised her with visible emotion. Then they went off to the side as the trainer prepared the next three dogs for the exercise. They drank some water and enjoyed the sense that, perhaps for the first time, they were a united pack.

They relaxed for a while as the exercise carried on. The joy of dogs coming to their owners was heartwarming to watch. Once the last handler came back out of the woods, the second phase started.

"This time, your dog stays here and you're the one moving into the woods," the trainer explained, "you'll go 500 meters along the same path they've been on before. You'll stay at that spot for ten minutes. Then you'll move another 500 meters straight ahead. Leave plenty of clues for your dog: drag and stomp your feet as you walk, so your scent is everywhere on that path."

If the last exercise caused anxiety, this one amplified it into true tension. But by then, the owners had started to trust the trainer and, making sure their dog's fluorescent harness was properly secured, marched off into the woods.

This exercise took much longer – after their ten-minute wait, Alec had started off in the wrong direction and Emily had to pull him back. They were so careful to stomp through the woods that their legs got tired as if they were on a stair machine at the gym.

The wait for Maggie to find them was agonizing. Though the woods were calm and beautiful, both Alec and Emily felt like they were writing an important exam they'd forgotten to study for.

Soon enough, Maggie's white coat flickered through the woods – they had never seen her so completely focused. Her nose was almost touching the ground, and she was studiously investigating every leaf and rock in her path before moving forward. Though their hearts leapt when they saw her, they tried to stay quiet until she noticed them.

A quick glance up from the ground showed Maggie that her owners were in sight. She let out an excited bark and sprinted the last few meters towards them, and the joy of reunion washed over all three of them.

They waited a while in the woods before joining the others heading back to the clearing. As they walked through the woods, dogs and owners stepping in perfect harmony, Emily felt radiant and knew they'd made the right decision in coming here. Alec looked around and felt as if he finally understood what a dog truly was.

Maggie seemed different, too, as if she'd grown in the few hours they'd been training. She walked with a confident step, finally aware of all she could achieve with her innate instincts and powerful senses.

MAGGIE'S HAPPY ENDING

The workshops continued that day and the next. During their breaks the family enjoyed their beautiful surroundings and de-stressed a little bit too.

The weekend was a turning point for Maggie and the whole family. They finally understood their Poodle, her needs and inner world, and that made rules and training much easier to follow. Maggie's anxieties melted away as she got plenty of exercise and opportunities to use her newly discovered passion for tracking.

With continuous training, work, and the occasional dog-friendly holiday, the family became closer than ever. In fact, they became a true pack.

STEP 10:
KNOWING YOURSELF, KNOWING YOUR DOG

Discovering the possibilities, and enjoying the journey

The Origin of 'Knowing Yourself, Knowing Your Dog'

Until now, the cubs' entire world has been a warm, comfortable den. In the den they've been fed, cleaned and protected by their sweet mom Channy and their dad, Stevo.

Today, everything is changing for these little cubs. They're embarking on their first adventure, leaving the den. Stevo watches them with a smile on his face as they waddle out, some shy, some confident, all amazed at so many new things – soft grass, bright sun, and oh, so many new wolves!

Stevo remembers the first time he left the den. So much has changed since then, but at heart he's still the same precocious spirit: constantly trying and striving for more, never satisfied with mediocrity, always throwing himself into a life of adventure. Though he'd felt fear, doubt, and discomfort throughout his life, he'd never let it hold him back.

Perhaps it was his destiny to be here, the leader of a successful pack, with an incredible partner and a litter of perfect little cubs. He was certainly gifted with energy, tenacity and bravery from birth. On the other hand, he was the one who kept taking leaps of faith – following Channy, leading the pack to this territory, and rescuing his love were all moments that had shaped his life, and ones that fate hadn't handed to him on a silver platter. He'd earned those things, just as he'd earned the title of Alpha Wolf.

He tapped his paws lightly on the ground to try and recreate what his cubs were experiencing, touching the grass for the first time. Their shock and awe at the simple sensation was adorable to watch. He looked up from them to Channy, and his heart was beating with the same intensity it had when he first saw her, and when he found her after losing her.

As the cubs frolicked around the grass outside the den, the other pack members arrived to meet them. The little ones didn't seem frightened at all. Channy beamed with pride as they confidently met their elders.

The biggest boy marched up to Lesus and said, "Hi! What's your name? Let's wrestle!"

Lesus burst out laughing, "I think I found the next Alpha over here!"

Channy shot a glance at Stevo and they both chuckled. It was suddenly obvious they needed to teach the cubs a few submissive postures before they got too full of themselves.

There were some strong personalities in the litter. However, the main reason the cubs were so relaxed in front of all these strangers was that their parents were so confident. It was hard to imagine, with two imposing figures like Channy and Stevo on guard, that anyone could approach the little ones with bad intentions.

Then there was the attitude of the pack. It wasn't like the strict, tense environment where Stevo had grown up, where the pressure was always on to behave properly or you might step on someone's toes and get a bite for your trouble. In Stevo's pack, he'd created true harmony, and everyone felt secure in their position. Rather than being threatened and defensive, the pack was always helping each other, focused on making life as easy as possible by working together.

He'd made the pack the best it could be, and their new arrivals would bring this family even closer together.

The Essence of 'Knowing Yourself, Knowing Your Dog'

As a puppy you were my student, as an adult, my teacher.

This sentence perfectly describes how a dog's presence influences our lives. It's the essence of our journey.

It's a pivotal moment when you realize dogs are simply better at coping with life than we humans are. You'd think we'd be the superior species, here at the (self-proclaimed) top of the animal kingdom. And yet when you look at it squarely, the average dog's ability to overcome difficult situations and enjoy every moment would give any Zen guru a run for their money.

At the beginning of our lives, humans and dogs are actually very similar. Kids and puppies are curious about everything, observing the world relentlessly, easily surprised and delighted by the most insignificant (to us) sights or sounds. They meet every moment with enthusiasm, accepting every experience as a precious gift.

We "adults" often make the mistake of trying to understand dogs at a distance. We study their behavior through books, courses, conferences and scientific papers. When we want to change their behavior, we might mistakenly believe there's some holy set of instructions, and if we follow the right tutorial, the dog will magically be corrected.

This overly cerebral approach takes us away from our dog's – and our – true essence. So, how do we connect with and truly understand our furry friends?

Observation would be one approach. We could watch them, with an open mind, for hours on end. Not only is this a bit time consuming, but it only takes us so far. We may see their actions, but not their intentions. To truly see things from their perspective, we must let go of our own point of view and allow ourselves to experience the canine universe: going from sympathy to empathy.

Every word in this book aims to help you develop empathy for your dog, a sense of deep understanding and connection. This not only strengthens your relationship with them but allows you to fully enjoy their company too.

If you've come this far and you're still with us, congratulations! You're well on your way to living in perfect harmony with your furry friend. If you've been paying careful attention to our instructions and have diligently followed the exercises, all that remains is for you to take the final step: take care of yourself. You are your dog's leader, the center of their universe, and they'll always mirror your emotions. So invest as much care and energy into your own wellbeing as you have into your pack's happiness.

If perfect harmony feels like a far-off goal, don't worry. Sometimes life gives us the dog we've always wanted, and other times we find ourselves with an animal who tests us, whose character and behavior makes us question ourselves.

The challenging dog may be an even greater blessing, as they make you confront your own bad habits, break your old patterns, and force you to grow into a better version of yourself. And once you overcome those hurdles and achieve a peaceful, happy home, you can feel deeply proud of yourself for making that transformation.

So, whether you're just beginning your journey to a happy pack or you're deep in the middle of it, thank yourself for doing the work. From today you'll see the world from a new perspective – not just through your human eyes, but through the eyes of a dog. What a breath of fresh air that will be!

The same route you follow when walking your dog will look fresh and new. When your furry friend suddenly stops and, beaming with happiness, shows you a particularly interesting leaf or stick, barking "Hey, look what I found!" there will be a magic moment.

You'll shrug off the tired old reaction of "Come on, let's go, we're running late," and instead come over to them and exclaim, "Wow! What did you find? That's amazing! You really are a special dog, you know!"

'Knowing Yourself, Knowing Your Dog' Case Study

Now it's time to write your story!

_____

_____

_____

_____

_____

_____

_____

_____

_____

_____

_____

_____

_____